Lovebirds and their Colour Mutations

Lovebirds and their Colour Mutations

Jim Hayward

*Photographs and Illustrations
by the author*

BLANDFORD PRESS
Poole · New York · Sydney

First published in the U.K. 1979 by Blandford Press,
Link House, West Street,
Poole, Dorset, BH15 1LL

Copyright © 1979 Blandford Press Ltd.

Reprinted in this edition 1987

Distributed in the United States by
Sterling Publishing Co, Inc.,
2 Park Avenue, New York, NY 10016

Distributed in Australia by
Capricorn Link (Australia) Pty Ltd
PO Box 665, Lane Cove, NSW 2066

British Library Cataloguing in Publication Data

Hayward, Jim
Lovebirds and their colour mutations.
1. Lovebirds
I. Title
636.6'865   SF473.L6

ISBN 0 7137 1981 8

Filmset by Keyspools Ltd, Golborne, Lancs.
Printed and Bound in Great Britain by
Butler & Tanner Ltd.,
Frome and London

Contents

Foreword

Lovebird species are widely distributed throughout the continent of Africa, with the exception of one which originates from the Island of Madagascar. These lively little parrots are fascinating to keep and provide, for both the novice and experienced aviculturalist, a satisfaction and challenge that few other species can offer. Lovebirds have long been extremely popular as aviary birds and, with all the new colour mutations appearing on the scene, demand for them has increased tremendously over the past few years.

This book presents a comprehensive study of the lovebird and, I am sure, will be of tremendous benefit to the novice, as well as the competent fancier. The information is derived from Jim Hayward's own experience in keeping lovebirds, which makes the information of practical value to the reader. His expertise in the breeding of the Masked and the Peach Faced Mutations will be invaluable to all those aviculturalists who are in the process of trying to establish the various colours. The discussion on the colour expectations resulting from the various pairings will assist those interested in these species. The photographs, I am sure, will tempt many a newcomer to try his hand at breeding lovebirds.

The sections on breeding and health problems will give the reader a clear and thorough basic knowledge of the problems, how to diagnose these and how best to resolve them.

Dr W. D. Russell
Bryanston Veterinary Clinic
South Africa. February 1979.

Introduction

Lovebirds (genus *Agapornis*) are an interesting group of parrots (family Psittaciformes) originating from the continent of Africa and the Island of Madagascar. The genus comprises nine species three of which are sexually dimorphic, the Red-Faced, Abyssinian and Madagascar. The four eye-ringed species are the Masked, Fischer's, Nyasa and Black-Cheeked. The Peach-Faced species is an intermediate one (between the sexually dimorphic and the eye-ringed). They possess some traits of the former group but are not sexually dimorphic, while their appearance resembles the eye-ringed more closely but lacks the bare eye ring. Black-Collared Lovebirds, the least known of the genus, remain birds of some mystery and do not fit into the above groups being individualistic in their habits and appearance.

Most taxonomists are of the opinion that the sexually dimorphic group are the more ancient and are the root stock from which the other species evolved. Some think that the closest relations of the lovebirds are the Hanging Parrots, which do have similar nesting habits, carrying lining material into their nests; others consider that they are more closely allied to the Ringneck (Indian and African), the King parrot and the Eclectus Group.

Lovebirds are, and always have been, popular with aviculturists throughout the world for many reasons. The commoner species are ideal for newcomers to birdkeeping being reasonably easily bred, hardy, active and vividly coloured. A large aviary is not required to achieve success. Those species which are rarer in confinement are a challenge for even the most advanced parrot breeder. The growing number of colour mutations is of great interest and will become more readily available in future. There is always the possibility of a completely new colour appearing in a nest of young which should, by their parentage, be normal.

Lovebirds gained their name from their habit of sitting closely together in pairs (not necessarily true pairs) and from the belief that if one of a pair died the other, due to grief, quickly followed suit. Although they are in some cases rather difficult to re-mate, the more logical explanation is that the first one to die had an infection which was passed on to the other.

Hen lovebirds carry out incubation on their own, the cocks being the providers and helping to feed the young. Although they spend time in the nest, individual cocks vary in this habit, some of them

7

roosting in the nest and others not.

Do be warned that these birds are not always as affectionate as their name implies but can be very pugnacious among themselves and other genera. For this reason it is most sensible to house breeding pairs separately rather than in a colony. Immature birds can be kept together in small groups but, even so, care should be taken to remove any offenders who breech the peace before serious damage is done.

To my family and my friends in aviculture throughout the world

1   Suitable Housing

Some species, such as the Peach-Faced (which are the most hardy) the Masked, Fischer's and Abyssinians, can be kept outside all the year round with little risk. They should, of course, be provided with a nestbox in which to roost, or a small and cosy enclosed shelter.

There is a higher risk with Black-Cheeked, Nyasas and Madagascars so these are best kept inside in a frost-free shed (in as large a flight cage as possible) through the coldest months of late autumn, winter and early spring. They can be put out for breeding through spring, summer and early autumn. Alternately, they can have access to an outside flight into which they can be allowed to fly on suitably mild days. Of the three species, I have found the Black-Cheeked are probably hardiest, the other two are more prone to lung trouble when subjected to cold, damp and draughty conditions.

Red-Faced lovebirds are the least hardy of the family and (especially with the unpredictable British climate) should be kept inside in flight cages or, preferably, in interior aviaries with access to well-sheltered exterior flights in which they can be allowed to fly on warm days.

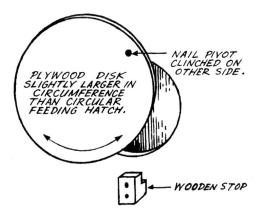

A useful and easily made feeding hatch which requires no hinges.

It is most convenient to build outside flights in ranges with a service passage along the back or front to prevent birds escaping while they are being fed, cleaned out etc. In Britain, it is advisable to construct the aviaries in such a way that they can be protected from bitter weather from the north and east also, if possible, protected from the prevailing westerly winds leaving the front of the aviaries

Range of lovebird flights with fence serving as one side of the service corridor.

exposed to the more beneficial weather from the south.

The front of the aviaries can be boarded in up to three feet high, which will stop draughts chilling birds that are feeding on the floor and prevent cats from attempting to catch any birds climbing up the wire. The top of the aviaries should be partially covered in, preferably at both ends of the flight, to afford protection from the weather, and the front can also be filled in about nine inches from the top to protect any birds which may end up roosting there through night fright.

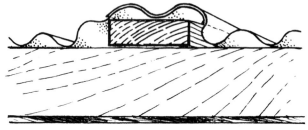

A strip of battening under overlapping joints of PVC roof sheeting helps prevent irritating drips.

It is a wise but expensive practice to double wire the partitions between the flights to prevent toes being bitten between neighbouring pairs and young. The floor can be covered with clean gravel which may be skimmed out and replaced as need be.

To keep rats from digging into the aviary, tack on a strip of wire mesh, approximately 460 mm (18 in) wide, to the bottom runner, lay back the adjacent turf and bury the mesh under it. If the aviary is surrounded with a buried skirt of mesh in this way the rats cannot bite through it, at least during a single night. Keep the sides of the aviary clear of any bits and pieces which vermin could hide beneath, they dislike working in the open and dig their burrows under cover at night.

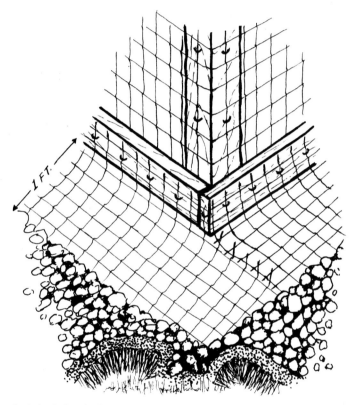

A method of excluding vermin by burying wire mesh adjacent to the sides of the flights.

Try to construct the aviary in such a way as to keep as much woodwork as possible covered by wire mesh to prevent the birds chewing it, which they will do to provide themselves with nesting material.

A 12 mm (0·5 in) dowel rod is ideal for perching and does not

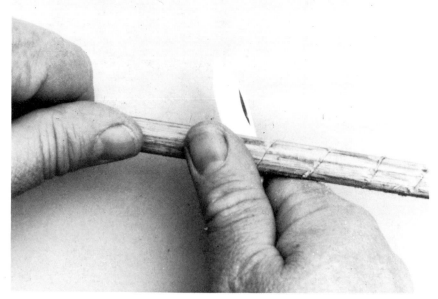

Scoring a spiral on perches with a knife ensures a firm grip for the mating birds.

clutter up the small flights as do odd shaped natural branches. To provide a good grip for the bird's feet (which is essential for successful copulation), the perches should be spiralled with a deep cut using a sharp penknife or scored by dragging the teeth of a saw down their length. Place the perches in a position which gives the birds enough room to copulate and fix them securely.

Breeding flights can be fairly small, say, 410 mm (16 in) wide. To save making lots of hinged doors budgerigar cage fronts can be stapled longways onto the aviary fronts so that the door in the cage fronts open upwards. The flights can be only 915 mm × 915 mm (3 ft × 3 ft) made with one inch by half inch welded mesh, standing on a framework three feet from the ground, and the roof covered in corrugated PVC. The advantages of small breeding flights are ease of catching, feeding and cleaning out. If the floor is made of wire it can be cleaned easily with a stiff brush, the droppings and wasted seed will go straight through the wire onto the ground so it can be swept up and disposed of.

It is a good idea to paint the aviary wire with black bituminous paint to retard rust and make it easier to see the birds. A paint roller works very well on wire mesh.

Range of smaller lovebird flights.

Woodwork can be treated with a non-poisonous wood preservative. Do not put the birds back into the flights before the paint and preservative are thoroughly dry.

2   Feeding

The feeding routine should be carried out every morning and afternoon or evening. The basic food mixture suitable for lovebirds consists of 50% canary and 50% white millet, with liberal amounts of panicum millet, Japanese millet and a small amount of sunflower seed added, more when there are young in the nest.

Soaked sunflower seed is given during the warm months. Soaking overnight is sufficient to cause the seed kernel to swell. Care must be taken to swill away any sour water and wash the soaked seed before it is given. Germinated seeds are particularly favoured; the sunflower seed should be soaked over night, drained off, the receptacle covered and left to stand for one or two days, depending upon the temperature. The seed should be fed to the birds when the shoots are about a quarter to a half inch long and still white, after which they soon turn to leaf and stem. Millet sprays are given dry or soaked; when soaked they must be carefully washed as they stagnate much more quickly than sunflower seed.

It is not necessary to use hemp or niger, and the lack of it does not show in the bird's general condition and breeding ability I find.

Apple, as well as moistened brown bread, with a light sprinkling of vitamin and mineral powder should be offered to those species which enjoy it. Cuttlefish bone and grit in some form should be available at all times. Clean water must be given daily in a cup hung on the side of the flight, well away from overhead perches, in preference to a dish on the floor. Seed should be checked for quantity and blown out every morning and afternoon, possibly even more frequently if the nests are full of ravenous youngsters.

Care should be taken to ensure that the seed is of good quality and free of heavy accumulation of dust and dirt. The canary seed should be large, plump and shiny. If cracked, the sunflower seed should be plump, greyish white and have a nutty flavour. There should be no predominance of husks mixed in the seeds, nor seeds which are yellowish with dried up kernels, nor should they taste rank or bitter. Always purchase small sunflower seed if you can; the kernel is just as big in the small seed as it is in the larger in which latter case you are paying for more shell. The birds prefer white or striped sunflower seed to black which does give out a very strong purplish black dye when soaked and stains the hands of the bird keeper.

Chinese millet sprays are usually cheaper, smaller, generally well filled with seed, and therefore more economical to use than are the large Italian sprays.

15

It is commonsense, of course, not to give frozen greenstuff and wildfood (greenstuff which is still frozen can cause scouring) nor greenstuff which has come from road verges or places where crop spraying has been carried out. It is important not to give apple late in the day during freezing weather to those birds which are outside.

Seeding grasses are enjoyed as food and appreciated as nesting material. Chickweed and shepherd's purse can be given. Willow is also appreciated as a food as well as for nest construction.

(1) Madagascar Cock

(2) Madagascar Hen

(3) Red-faced (true pair)

(4) Abyssinian (true pair)

(5) Black-collared (Zenker's left; Swindern's right)

(6) Black-cheeked

(7)   Nyasas (true pair and young bird)

(8)   Lutino Red-faced (left) and Lutino Nyasa (right)

(9) Fischer's

(10) Yellow (dilute) Fischer's

(11) Masked

(12) Blue Masked

(13) Yellow (dilute) Masked

(14) White (dilute blue) Masked

(15) Peach-faced

(16) Pied Peach-faced

(17)   Yellow (derived from Pied) Peach-faced

(18)   Pastel Blue (semi-blue) Peach-faced

(19) Pied Pastel Blue (Pied semi-blue) Peach-faced

(20) Buttermilk (derived from Pied semi-blue) Peach-faced

(21)   Golden Cherry (American dilute) Peach-faced in sunlight

(22)   Golden Cherry (American dilute) Peach-faced in shade

(23) Silver Cherry (American dilute semi-blue) Peach-faced

(24) Pied Golden Cherry (Pied American dilute) Peach-faced

(25)   Pied Silver Cherry (Pied dilute semi-blue) Peach-faced (immature bird)

(26)   Olive (double dark factor) Peach-faced

(27) Pied Olive Peach-faced (immature bird)

(28) Jade (single dark factor) Peach-faced (left) and Normal Peach-faced (right)

(29) Lutino Peach-faced

(30) Cream Lutino Peach-faced (immature bird)

(31) Cinnamon Peach-faced

(32) Future possibilities if true White-faced Blues exist. (Left to right: double dark factor White-faced Blue, Albino, single dark factor White-faced Blue and Pied White-faced Blue.)

3   Basic Genetics

In the nineteenth century it was demonstrated by the biologist Mendel that there are definite rules which govern genetic inheritance throughout the world of living things. By crossbreeding plants with contrasting physical characteristics definite patterns of inheritance emerged. These rules of Mendelism hold true for members of the animal kingdom and so we can use them to predetermine the colour expectations when one mutant colour is crossed with another or with the normally coloured bird of that species.

A *mutant* is a specimen occuring which differs from the normal, not necessa‌ ly only in colour, but perhaps in external or internal physical form‌ ‌ may have been caused by various factors such as change of i‌ ‌ ‌estors' native habitat, food supply, or perhaps just an ‌ the cells of the creature when first conceived.

‌ occur in captivity as well as in the wild, even more ‌ ‌ inbreeding and linebreeding often employed by ‌ ‌ases latent mutant factors which may have lain ‌ generations.

‌f a species need not necessarily be a good thing ‌ wild as it may, for example, make them more ‌tors, or unattractive to their opposite sex. ‌liminate, in the wild, any mutant which would ‌ species' survival. Those mutant specimens
th‌ ‌ay develop into new species or sub-species
whic‌ evolution operates. Some mutant factors are
lethal ‌ entrated. Although some lethal mutants are
known ‌ canaries, fortunately none have so far been
discover‌

Th‌ ‌inant and *recessive* can be explained best by
examp‌ ‌e, a Normal (green) Masked lovebird is
dom‌ ‌ked lovebird, and the Blue is recessive to the
N‌ ‌at if they are paired together their progeny,
al‌ ‌ same colour as the dominant Normal, will be
‌ ‌entage of specimens of the recessive blue
‌d they are paired to: a Normal which had one
‌l Blue; or to a Normal which has inherited the
‌ing one or both Normal-looking parents which
‌ormal crossed with Blue.)
‌ch are visually of the dominant colour but able to
‌ctor for the recessive colour to their progeny are
‌ *split* for the recessive colour. *Split* is denoted by an

oblique sign, for example:

Normal Masked/Blue Masked

i.e., Normal Masked (in appearance) split

(able to produce) Blue Masked

Sex-linkage refers to the phenomenon in which the colour of the progeny depends on their sex. (The mutant colours, in this case, are sex determined.) Although cocks can be split for a sex-linked colour, hens cannot be as they are either visually of the sex-linked colour or completely normal.

With dominant and recessive colours the sex of the parents has no bearing whatsoever on the colouration of the resulting young.

The *dark factor* works in a different way from all the other mutants; it is partially dominant but is lessened in strength when birds possessing the factor are paired with birds lacking it. It can deepen the mutant and normal colours by two definite tones, these are referred to as *single dark factor* and *double dark factor*.

The *pied factor* is referred to as *single pied factor* and *double pied factor*, but this represents the ability which the bird has to reproduce its variety rather than a differing shade or lesser and greater amount of variegation.

Definite percentages of each colour expected from the pairings is not given as this varies greatly from nest to nest. With pairings that produce a multiple of colours and splits a number of nests may need to be bred before a single specimen of the desired colour is produced, alternately the very first nest of young may all be of the elusive colour for which you are breeding.

If we wish to perpetuate the new colours we must learn their pattern of inheritance by keeping records of breeding results. Sometimes the problems in fostering a new colour are very great and the colour is lost or only established after a long struggle.

As long as the specimens are strong, healthy birds then *inbreeding* or *line-breeding* may be used to speed up the process of establishing a strain of the new colour. Remember that in so doing the faults as well as the virtues of the original ancestor may be magnified in the progeny to a very great extent, so be sure to use only the best specimens for this purpose.

Faults such as distortion of form, infertility, feather abnormalities, hens which lay small clutches of eggs, birds which are poor parents, cocks which are pugnacious with their young, and so on could be magnified so as to prevent headway being made in the building of a strain if inbreeding and line-breeding are used indiscriminately.

Inbreeding is the term used to describe the pairing together of brother and sister, father and daughter or mother and son. If particular characteristics of one of a pair of birds are to be perpetuated, the young most favouring that parent (which we shall call the *key bird*) should be paired back to it. In turn their young are scrutinised for the opposite sex bird most like the key bird (which as well as being its parent is also its grandparent). This bird is paired back to the key bird and the sequence repeated as many times as necessary, as long as no degeneration is evident. By using this method of breeding, batches of young will be produced which are as alike as peas in a pod.

Finally a bird will be produced which is better than the key bird. This can then be used as another key bird to head its own line and hopefully produce even better progeny.

By using inbreeding young recessives can be produced from a single recessive in the second generation, for example:

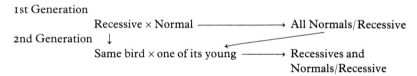

1st Generation

Recessive × Normal ⟶ All Normals/Recessive

2nd Generation ↓

Same bird × one of its young ⟶ Recessives and Normals/Recessive

Linebreeding is the term referring to the pairing together of cousins, uncles and nieces, aunts and nephews, half-brothers and half-sisters and even further distantly related stock.

It is a fact, provided the initial stock is sound, that more stable and consistent results are obtained by using for breeding those birds which are slightly related rather than completely unrelated stock which differs drastically in appearance and character.

4 The Lovebird species and their colour mutations

Sexually Dimorphic Species

Three species of lovebirds are sexually dimorphic; this is to say the sexes can be easily distinguished by striking differences in plumage. Their hatchlings have white or greyish white down.

The sexually dimorphic species are the Madagascar, the Red-Faced and the Abyssinian; these are considered to be the most ancient members of the genus and the root stock from which the other species evolved.

Madagascar Lovebird *Agapornis cana cana*
Length 14 cm (5·5 in)

Madagascar or the Grey-headed Lovebirds are most diminutive members of the genus and are widespread in all but the central plateau area of the island they are named after. They have also been introduced, with mixed success, into several of the small islands in the Indian Ocean; these being Mauritius and Rodriguez in the Mascarene Islands, in the Seychelles on the Island of Mahé, Comoro and Mafia Islands and the island of Zanzibar.

Preferring woodland of an open nature, rather than dense forest, they are to be seen in large flocks; there they live off the wild seeding grasses and make pests of themselves by raiding the cultivated grain and rice crops.

These lovebirds have a very small bill in comparison with the other members of their family, consequently they are particularly fond of small seeds like panicum, Japanese millet, canary and the tiny seeding grasses such as poa annua. The sunflower seed they do have should be as small as that which is given to British finches.

The sub-species *Agapornis cana ablectanea* inhabits the parched and barren area in the south-west of Madagascar and differs from the nominate race in having the green areas darker and the grey areas cleaner and brighter.

Appearance
With pearl grey head, neck and breast, lime green belly, laurel back and wings, green tail barred with black, grey bill and feet, the cock Madagascar certainly is a smart little chap and contrasts strongly with his rather dowdy but nonetheless neat little wife.

37

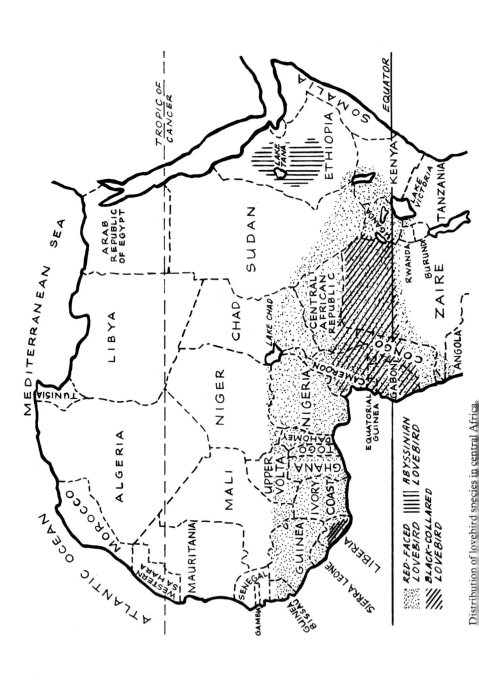

Distribution of lovebird species in central Africa.

38

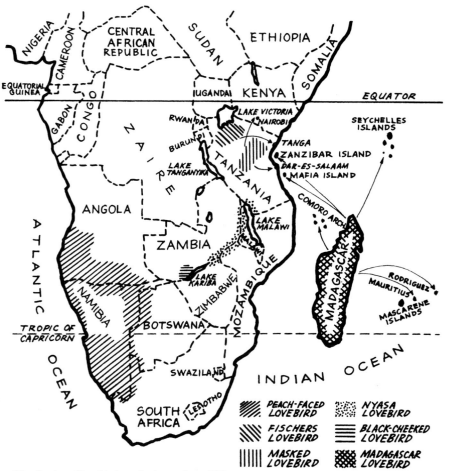

Distribution of lovebird species in southern Africa.

Hen Madagascars lack the grey plumage and the black underwing coverts possessed by the cocks. Immatures can be sexed easily as the young cocks show black underwing coverts like those of their fathers, and possess the grey areas though with a greenish cast.

Breeding
In the wild state they nest in hollow tress. The hen makes a pad on which to lay her four to six eggs; the pad being made from strips of whittled bark, leaves, and other materials which she carries into the hollow tucked under her rump feathers. The cock has a twittering

39

song during the breeding season and is rather subject to being henpecked by his shrewish wife.

Though in general these birds could not be considered prolific nor very hardy in confinement, being susceptible to lung trouble in cold and foggy weather, they have been and are fairly frequently bred so that it is possible that with patience a free breeding strain could be founded.

Most birds are very nervous and erratic when confined to cages and are liable to dash themselves against the ceiling and walls. For this reason they should have a secluded inside flight with access to a well sheltered outer one so that they can be kept in during periods of bad weather.

In confinement they will breed in a nestbox which should be made appropriately smaller than those for the larger lovebirds, bearing in mind their nesting habits and comparative size. They do not line out the sides of the nest nor make a domed structure and are, in fact, just as likely to throw out anything which is in the box as they are to carry material in. This being the case, some crumbled, well-rotted wood mixed with an amount of fine sand should be given as a base to stop the eggs rolling around, if the hen is inclined towards the former habit. Willow should be available for those birds that require it.

As they are nervous birds, they resent interference and once breeding is underway it is wise to stifle curiosity and leave the nest alone. In Britain these lovebirds usually come into breeding condition in late summer or autumn.

Madagascars appreciate greenfood and apple, a vitamin and mineral supplement can be smeared on the latter. A little brown bread and milk can also be offered, especially when there are young in the nest.

Many years ago Madagascars were commonly available in Britain. This, sadly, is not the case now, of course, but as a number were offered for sale prior to the imposition of 1976 importation restrictions it is hoped that the owners of these birds are having success in establishing strains.

No mutations have been reported to my knowledge which is hardly surprising due to its low status in aviculture and previous lack of well-established breeding stock.

Red-Faced Lovebird *Agapornis pullaria pullaria*
Size 15 cm (5·9 in)

The Red-Faced Lovebird prefers lightly wooded savannah country but is to be found in a vast band of country stretching from Ethiopia in the east through central Africa to Sierra Leone and Guinea on the west coast. The sub-species *Agapornis pullaria ugandae* differs in having a paler blue rump and is to be found in the utmost eastern end of the region.

In their equatorial habitat, Red-Faced lovebirds live on seeding grasses, fruit, shoots of foliage, berries and figs; they also raid ripening crops. In captivity they eat the usual seed mixture, greenfoods, and are particularly fond of apple. Their habit of roosting upside down like the Hanging Parrots is frequently referred to. However, a friend in Britain tells me that his birds roost normally. In the wild they nest in arboreal termitaries burrowing right inside to make a hollow in which to rear their young. They prefer only those termitaries that are situated in the highest trees.

Breeding

These birds have been bred only rarely and spasmodically until recent times. There are a few reports of Red-Faced lovebirds being bred in the late 1800s to early 1900s in both Europe and America. However, the most well known and fully recorded breeding was by Mr Prestwich in Britain in the mid 1950s. After some false starts his first young fledged in the month of December. They were bred in a colony which was left in an outside aviary through the winter which was quite remarkable. In this case the nesting receptacles were small barrels rammed tight with peat to simulate termite nests.

In the late 1950s, a South African aviculturist bred Red-Faced lovebirds. The young were reared mainly on small seeds (i.e. millets and canary) and, notably, leaves of the Morning Glory plant. This time the nest used was made of a block of cork enclosed with wood on all sides except the front from where the birds excavated inwards.

A few years later, in the 1960s, a Danish breeder was successful, breeding them in a more conventional type of wooden nest box. One of the more unusual but staple items of the diet which the parents fed to their young was a daily and copious amount of mealworms.

Now, in recent years, the most businesslike, concerted and successful efforts at breeding these dainty birds must surely be those of Mr Coelho in Portugal using a modified version of the cork block idea. The improvement in using this material instead of peat is that the danger of the roof caving in on the nesting birds, eggs and young is eliminated.

In Britain, Mr Garfield has achieved success by using the cork nest and breeding inside in flight cages. The birds, the hen doing most of

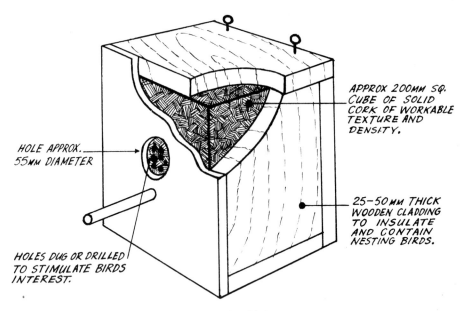

APPROX 200MM SQ. CUBE OF SOLID CORK OF WORKABLE TEXTURE AND DENSITY.

HOLE APPROX. 55MM DIAMETER

25-50MM THICK WOODEN CLADDING TO INSULATE AND CONTAIN NESTING BIRDS.

HOLES DUG OR DRILLED TO STIMULATE BIRDS INTEREST.

Suggested design for a cork nest for Red-faced lovebirds.

the work, took about three weeks to excavate a chamber and four eggs were laid. The young fledged at just under six weeks. The cork nest block must of course be enclosed with a wooden casing to prevent the nesting birds from going straight through the sides, bottom or top. The birds excavate a tunnel straight through the cork until they hit the back board then turn left, right or up to hollow out a small and cosy chamber roughly 10 cm (4 in) in width. Once the birds have used their nest a slice can be cut off the top to make a removable lid to facilitate nest inspection the following season. The tunnel and chamber should be packed with cork granules to make the birds work to gain entrance and stimulate their breeding instincts in the process. It is suggested a wooden nest could be made to simulate a tunnel and nest chamber as an experiment to see if this would be acceptable to the lovebirds. Various mixtures could be used as packing to stimulate the birds' curiosity and satisfy their need to dig, for example, earth, sand, rotten wood, peat, cork granules etc.

Appearance
Cock Red-Faced lovebirds are bright green, darker above, lighter below, faces and foreheads are red, tails are barred with black and marked with red, their rumps are blue, their irides are brown and

their bills red. The hens' faces are more orange than red.

Once again, they are easily sexed; the hen has green underwing coverts while the cock has underwing coverts and bend of the wing black. The youngsters differ from the adults in having yellow faces and light brown bills. Even at the fledgling age young cocks and hens show the same difference in coloration of the underwing coverts as do the adults.

Red-Faced lovebirds were probably the first of all the lovebirds to be imported into Britain; evidence of them being kept as pets dates back to the sixteenth century. They were the most commonly available species before the war but are seldom come by now; those imported in recent years probably came originally from Portuguese nationals returning from Angola when that country gained its independence.

Their voices are softer and more twittering than most of their relatives and their flight is buoyant and light.

Red-Faced lovebirds are difficult, if not impossible, to acclimatise to conditons in Britain. Recent breeding successes here have been with birds kept in large indoor flight cages. It is doubtful that they would ever become completely hardy.

There are reports of both Pied and Lutino mutations but no confirmation that these colours are firmly established. Recent breeding results in Europe prove the Lutino to be a recessive mutation.

Abyssinian Lovebird *Agapornis taranta*
Size 16.5 cm (6·4 in)

The Abyssinian Lovebird, also known as the Black-Winged Lovebird, inhabits the highlands and mountainous regions of Ethiopia, in some areas where the altitude exceeds 2,750 m (9,000 ft). In these areas, though daytime temperatures can pass 27°C (80°F) night temperatures can drop below freezing or the evergreen trees in which they roost can be made wet and dank by enveloping cloud. This would suggest that these birds are extremely hardy and able to withstand rigorous conditions and colder temperatures than the rest of the genus. (For some reason it is commonly found in aviculture that the cocks are less strong than the hens. If one of a pair is lost it is found more frequently to be the cock.)

Abyssinians in the wild state live on seeding grasses, fruits and berries and are most often found feeding among acacias, euphorbias, junipers (whose berries they appreciate) and the sycamore fig. Birds from the south-west of the range differ a little in having slighter bills than the rest of the population.

Breeding
They roost and also nest in the hollow limbs of trees; the hen carries strips of wood, bark, and so on, (tucked under her feathers) into the nest. This material is simply to line the bottom and is generally very sparse as an elaborate nest is not constructed; they are pad nesters. In confinement nest construction of any type is generally found to be non-existent so enough crumbled, rotted wood to form a base for the eggs to be laid on should be put in the nest.

Three to four eggs are usually laid and incubated for a period of twenty-six days. According to breeders, the hatchlings have a very short white to greyish white down which is just perceptible but increases in density as the birds progress. They stay in the nest for almost seven weeks, resembling their mothers on fledging (apart from their bills, which are yellow darkly streaked from the base with black.)

Appearance
First imported into Britain in 1909, these large and sturdily built lovebirds are very handsome. The cock is vivid green, darker on the upper parts; forehead, lores and the ring of feathers around the eye are red. The tail is green, boldly barred with black which is also the colour of the underwing coverts, flight and secondary feathers. The colour of the secondary feathers has given the species its other name—Black-Winged Lovebird. Feet are grey, and iris brown. The bill is rose red, paler at its tip.

Hens lack the red forehead and eye ring of the cocks. The underwing coverts vary quite a lot between individuals and, although usually dark green with an admixture of black, can sometimes be just as black as those of the cocks.

Youngsters resemble the hens, but the immature cocks have black underwing coverts. Through speaking to breeders of this species I find there is a predominance of young cocks being bred at the present time.

Despite their increasing popularity Abyssinians are not all that easily bred. They should be provided with the usual type of lovebird nest of an appropriate size, set up under cover in a secluded corner of the aviary. Damper weather in spring and autumn seems to be conducive to breeeding.

They will eat the same food as other lovebirds: canary, millet, sunflower, greenfood, apple and so on. They are said to enjoy dried figs. In the wild, as has been mentioned previously, they feed on juniper berries which are apparently high in vitamins of the B group, so these vitamins added in some form to their diet should prove an embellishment and bring about more satisfactory results.

Blue mutants of this species were once thought to exist but nothing seems to have been heard of them recently.

Black-Collared Lovebird *Agapornis swinderniana*
Size 13 cm (5 in) *swinderniana*

Either rare or extremly evasive, Swindern's Black-Collared Lovebird, least known of the genus, lives in the forests of Liberia. Some dead specimens are reported to have been brought to Europe by explorers in the late nineteenth century, but, supposedly, no living specimens have so far been imported due to their specialised feeding habits.

It seems strange in comparison with other exotics that the difficulties of importing and the provision of diet for such a bird have not been overcome, particularly as it was known in Europe at least a hundred years before most of the eye-ringed lovebirds were imported into Britain.

They are said to be busy among fruit trees and oil-palms in small groups but both Swindern's (the nominate race) and Zenker's live in the dense evergreen forests which are to be found in both their habitats. Apparently they can live for only a few days without the supply of a particular kind of fig which must be in a fresh condition, and from these they extricate the numerous tiny seeds. It is also possible that they are partly insectivorous.

In appearance they differ from all the other lovebirds in having black bills and yellow irides. No sexual dimorphism is apparent. They are mainly green, darker above and lighter below. The tail is marked with reddish orange barred with black and the rump is a rich violet blue. There is a black collar and the neck below it is yellow. The young differ from the adults in lacking the black collar and in having grey bills and brown irides.

Nesting habits remain a mystery but it is suggested that they may nest in termitaries in trees like their cousins the Red-Faced lovebirds, in whose company they are found, or in the roots of tree ferns.

They like to be near water as they need to wash off the remnants of their sticky diet. They have been observed drinking liquid mud

45

which may provide a particular mineral they need.

The sub species, Zenker's Black-Collared Lovebird *Agapornis swinderniana zenkeri* is found in the Congo, Cameroon, Gabon and Central African Republic. It differs from Swindern's in having the yellow collar beneath the black collar replaced by a brownish orange and this collar also encroaches onto the throat and breast.

It apparently feeds among the cultivated crops of rice, maize and sesame seed; if this is so it may not be as specialised as Swindern's and we may yet see some imported.

Agapornis swinderniana emini is similar to Zenker's and is to be found in Western Uganda.

The Eye-Ringed species

The Eye-Ringed species show no sexual dimorphism. They share the same habit of constructing bulky domed nests within their chosen nesting sites. Their natural habitat is confined to relatively small areas in comparison with most other members of the genus. Taking into account the limited geographical area of these habitats, the effect on these species should be considered if they are altered by man or natural calamities and the value of aviary bred strains appreciated.

Sexing these species in general is very difficult and proof of sex of a pair can only be assured by the existence of fertile eggs. Mature cocks are generally built slimmer than hens, and mature hens are more squat and wider in the abdomen. All the species have naked white eye-rings which give them a cheeky, clownish appearance.

Head of Nyasa.

46

Head of Black-cheeked.

The Black-Cheeked is basically the same bird as the Nyasa apart from the colour of its head and upper breast; the size of body, colour of iris, colour and size of bill are all identical. Likewise with the Masked and Fischer's, they too are comparative in size, the irides are the same, so too are their waxy red bills.

The four species all carry their nesting materials in their bills.

Black-Cheeked Lovebird *Agapornis nigrigenis*
Size 13·5 cm (5·3 in)

The Black-Cheeked Lovebird (in 1904) was the first of the Eye-Ringed Lovebirds to be imported into Britain. In the 1920's Black-Cheeked lovebirds were widely bred and said to be prolific, (unfortunately this is not the case at present). After many thousands were trapped by unscrupulous dealers, in 1929 the British authorities in Northern Rhodesia (now Zambia) brought about a ban on the export of these birds. For the Black-Cheeked lovebird the danger of decimation and ultimate extinction was very real, as they are restricted in their habitat to the smallest natural area of all their genus. The extent of this is from the tributaries of the Zambesi in south west Zambia, southwards to the vicinity of the Victoria Falls in north west Zimbabwe. In the wild they feed on the usual fare of seeding grasses, buds, berries and fruits; they also scavenge among the sorghum crops.

Black-Cheeked lovebirds kept in aviaries prefer the smaller seeds: canary, white millet, Japanese millet and panicum, with very little

47

sunflower. They like apple, on which can be given vitamin and mineral powder, moistened brown bread, seeding chickweed and seeding grasses. The latter, together with the long thin supple twigs of the weeping willow, are preferred for nestbuilding. They do not favour the thicker branches of willow which the Masked and Peach-Faced lovebirds are quite pleased to whittle and utilize.

Breeding
Black-Cheeked lovebirds are reasonably hardy, but they are badly affected where conditions are extremely wet, foggy and cold. They nest in much the same way as do the Masked by adding continually to the material in the nest box, usually until the nesting chamber is level with the entrance hole. When things reach this state it is best to clean everything out and start them off anew by putting a twist of dry grass or a few used millet sprays in the bottom of the box. Do not use those sprays that have been on the floor of the aviary as these may introduce fodder mite into the nest.

Like the other eye-ringed lovebirds, the Black Cheeked are not confined to any rigid pattern with regard to breeding season but will go to nest whenever they are in breeding condition and, provided weather conditions are not too extreme, will raise young winter or summer. Sexes are alike in appearance, so the only way of being sure you have a true pair is when they produce fertile eggs. Their hatchlings are covered with a pinkish orange down; the fledglings are very attractive being smaller and only slightly duller in colouration compared with their parents. Their bills are pale orange fawn, redder at the tip, their irides are dark and they have a few dark flecks on their feet together with dark nails.

Colour
The Black-Cheeked are green, darker above and lighter beneath having an olive tinge to the backs of their heads. Their crowns and foreheads are a warm chestnut brown, cheek and throat are black and there is a roughly crescent shaped patch of apricot on the upper breast just beneath the throat. Their bills are red at the tip fading to pale pink at the base, they have a bare white eye-ring and their irides are fawn to brown. It is said that the coloration of the iris, brown or fawn, is an indicator of sex, though I have never found this to be so.

Unfortunately these birds have been crossed indiscriminately in the past with Masked, Nyasas and Peach-Faced, consequently hybrids abound. As breeding stock these should be avoided at all costs and discarded. (Lovebird hybrids, of course, are usually fertile).

Like the Nyasas, the Black-Cheeked have a needle sharp bill and piercing bite and will nip a piece of flesh from your fingers given half a chance.

In the past, a blue variety of this species has been advertised for sale but there is strong reason to believe that these were not true mutants within the species but had been acquired by crossing the normal Black-Cheeked with the Blue Masked; the first such cross would produce hybrids split for blue and then by pairing these birds together, or back to a Blue masked, a certain amount of blue hybrids would result. To eliminate the characteristics of the Masked altogether would take many years of back pairing to the pure Black-Cheeked involving ruthless culling of unsuitable young birds. It is debatable whether it would be worth the trouble.

Black-Cheeked lovebirds were quite rare a few years ago but recently a few are being offered for sale in Britain. It is to be hoped that they are pure bred and will prove to be as prolific as their ancestors were in the Britain of fifty and more years ago.

To establish strains of this bird would be extremely worthwhile. Birds with such small breeding territories in the wild (no matter how many they number) are always at risk of decimation whether it be through natural or man made catastrophies. From the point of view of preserving the species the more that thrive in aviaries around the world the better.

Nyasa Lovebird *Agapornis lilianae*
Size 13·5 cm (5·3 in)

The Nyasa Lovebird is to be found in a region straddling the borders of Zambia, Zimbabwe, Tanzania, Malawi and Mozambique. There they take over the nests of Weaver Birds for their breeding and roosting purposes, living off the land like their cousins, the Black-Cheeked, and occasionally marauding the cereal crops. Unlike most of the other species they prefer to live along river valleys rather than in wooded savannah.

Nyasas were first imported into Britain in 1926, at first they were mistaken for the Peach-Faced, which seems impossible to believe when picturing the contrasting physical characteristics and varying colouration of the two species.

The territories of *Lilianae* and *nigrigenis* do not overlap but these two species are so very much alike that they appear as colour varieties of the same bird. Nyasas are a slightly paler shade of sparkling green than Black-Cheeked. Their face, cheeks, crown, throat and forehead

49

are orange, (brighter on the forehead), there is a crescent-shaped patch of orange on the upper breast joining the throat. The head and breast of the Nyasa has the same pattern as that of the Black-Cheeked, just coloured differently. Bills and eyes are the same as is described for nigrigenis.

It is a common fallacy that the eyes of the Nyasas and Black-Cheeked are an indicator of sex, the iris being lighter or darker as the case may be. In fact the eyes of both sexes change becoming darker or lighter over a period of time.

Nyasas have also been subject to indiscriminate crossing with other species in the past when sufficient breeding stock was unobtainable. Apart from the more obvious pointers to an admixture of Masked, Fischer's or Peach-Faced blood, Nyasas of mongrel pedigree will show some blue in the rump. Both Nyasas and the Black-Cheeked have clear light green rumps when of pure blood.

Nyasas should be fed the same food as is recommended for the Black-Cheeked. They are supposed to be prolific breeders but I have not found them as resilient as the Black-Cheeked to cold, damp and foggy weather. They would be much better off inside for the winter and outside for breeding in spring, summer and early autumn.

They are quite good nest makers, sometimes making a dome. The clutch of, usually, four eggs hatch in twenty days and the hatchlings have a pinkish orange down. The fledglings are like their parents only smaller and slighlty duller, their irides are darker and their bills more orange.

In the late 1940s Nyasas were almost extinct as aviary birds in Britain. There are a number of people breeding them at the time of writing but they are a long way from being commonly available.

Sexing holds the usual problems and fertile eggs are the only proof of a true pair. Cocks can show a brighter orange forehead but this is by no means a hard and fast rule.

There is a very beautiful Lutino mutation of Nyasa which is golden yellow with white flights, orange head, pink iris and red pupil. The bill is the same as that of the normal and their feet and legs are pink. Unlike most Lutino mutations, which are sex-linked, Lutino Nyasas are recessive:

Pairing	Colour of Young
Lutino × Normal	All Normal/Lutino
Normal/Lutino × Normal/Lutino	Normals, Lutinos and Normals/Lutino
Normal × Normal/Lutino	Normals and Normals/Lutino
Lutino × Normal/Lutino	Normals/Lutino and Lutinos
Lutino × Lutino	All Lutinos

Unfortunately Lutino Nyasas defy probability and the law of averages and the splits produce a very low percentage of Lutinos with the result that, despite the fact that this colour first appeared in 1933 (in Adelaide, Australia) they are still very rare. In fact, from information gathered, breeders in America and Australia are either at a standstill or losing ground and the strains are degenerating. Although specimens were imported into Britain not many years after their first occurrence, attempts to establish them here have so far failed.

Blue Nyasas exist but it is not known whether they are of the true blue type of mutation or the semi-blue like the Pastel Blue Peach-Faced lovebirds.

Fischer's Lovebird *Agapornis fischeri*
Size 15 cm (5·9 in)

In an area spreading south from the shores of Lake Victoria, Fischer's Lovebird inhabits the savannah land of the high inland plateau of northern Tanzania which is vegetated by bush and sparse trees of a deciduous nature. There they feed upon the acacias and seeding grasses. In areas of human habitation they will raid the growing crops of maize and millet. Escaped aviary birds have successfully established themselves in a relatively smaller area of the southern part of Kenya.

In the late 1920s, due to concern at the vast amounts then being trapped for the cagebird trade a mass release of Fischer's lovebirds resulted in a successful colony establishing themselves in the port of Tanga, this being outside the bird's natural territory but the centre of the trade at the time. Apparently descendants of these birds still thrive in the area.

Breeding
In the wild they are colony breeders, carrying strips of bark, twigs, grass and so on in their bills into crevices in buildings, hollow trees, amid palm fronds or the communal nests of Weavers wherein they will construct their dometopped nests. They nest after rainy periods when the previously drought-ridden bush will provide enough extra food for the breeding pairs to rear their young.

The hen begins to incubate from the second or third egg and the young, which on hatching are covered with an orange down, fledge the nest between five and six weeks old. They return to the nest to

51

roost until the parents grow tired of them, wishing to go to nest again, and send them packing.

Though the borders of the territories of Fischer's and the Masked approach one another very closely there seemed to be no natural hybridisation as the species were thought to be kept apart by natural barriers. Recent evidence seems to show the contrary.

Fischer's lovebirds were first imported into Europe just after the First World War. In 1928 La Société d'Aclimatation de France awarded silver medals to the Marquis of Tavistock for the first breeding in Europe of both the Fischer's and Masked lovebird. The birds were imported at the end of the summer whereupon they were placed straight into an outside flight, the nest log being hung in the open flight with no protection from the weather. These birds went to nest in October and although the weather was bitter, some of the young were raised.

During the Second World War, as with most aviary birds in Britain, Fischer's lovebirds were reduced to a small and mostly degenerate stock but after fresh supplies were imported once more from the wild they have become widely bred, hardy and prolific; perhaps the most commonly bred apart from the Peach-Faced.

As an illustration of how good these birds can be at rearing young, an aviculturist related how, in recent years, a pair had raised a nest of young Rosellas (*Platycercus eximius*) which had been deserted by their own parents. Things were fine until the Rosellas fledged after which the foster parents would have no more to do with them and did in fact begin to attack them.

Colour

The colour of these lovebirds is mainly green, dark above and light below. Face, throat and forehead are reddish orange; the collar and upper portion of the breast are yellow; the tail is green marked with yellow and black. There is a blue patch on the rump, the bill is waxy red, the bare skin around the eye is white and the irides are brown. Youngsters differ from their parents in being duller coloured in general and in having dark streaks at the base of the bill.

Of added interest is the yellow Fischer's lovebird which is becoming very popular and gradually increasing in number.

The Yellow Fischer's lovebird is a recessive dilute mutation in which the green plumage is diluted to a lime colour – unfortunately the colour is rather blotchy in most specimens. The orange and yellow is clearer and brighter than in the normal and the flights are whitish. This mutant is parallel in form and genetic make-up with the Yellow

52

Masked; in fact it is highly probable that one has been obtained from the other through hybridisation.

Pairing	Colour of Young
Yellow × Yellow ⟶	All Yellows
Normal/Yellow × Yellow ⟶	Normals/Yellow and Yellows
Normal × Normal/Yellow ⟶	Normals and Normals/Yellow
Normal/Yellow × Normal/Yellow ⟶	Normals, Normals/Yellow and Yellows
Yellow × Normal ⟶	All Normals/Yellow

There is also a Lutino Fischer's lovebird which is clear bright yellow with reddish orange head, waxy red bill, white flights and a white (instead of blue) patch on the rump. Eyes are of course red, and feet pink. It is very rare, and, as it is reported to be recessive like the Lutino Nyasa, it is likely to be so for a long time to come.

A blue mutation is often reported. It is likely that this has been produced by hybridisation between Normal Fischer's and Blue Masked. The young, being hybrids split for blue, when paired together would produce a certain percentage of blue coloured hybrids. Specimens actually examined are suspected to be descendants of this cross.

Normal Fischer's lovebirds are rather rare in Australia and much sought after. Even so, there is on that continent a strain of recessive Black-Eyed Yellows which, unlike the Yellows to be commonly found in Britain, are a pure yellow colour. At least one yellow of this type exists in Britain and there are probably some in the USA.

There are increasing reports in Britain of pied specimens which, according to initial breeding results appear to be dominant.

Masked Lovebird *Agapornis personata*
Size 14·5 cm (5·7 in)

The Masked Lovebird comes from north east Tanzania and has also become established, through escaped and released birds, in Nairobi, Kenya and in the port of Dar Es Salaam. Colonies of birds originated in the latter case through a mass release of Maskeds in about 1928 because of the authorities' concern at the vast amounts being trapped and shipped out for the cage bird trade; this was about the same time as the mass release of Fischer's at Tanga already mentioned.

These birds are from the high inland plateau, a grassland which is wooded mainly with acacias; they live off the shrubs and seeding grasses in that region and will attack cereal crops when in their vicinity.

They are colony breeders, showing a preference for nesting in the large hollow baobab trees or in the crevices of buildings when in populated areas.

Appearance
The Masked are in my opinion the most attractive and appealing of all the lovebirds with their clownish looks. Their bills are a waxy red, and their heads are black, shading at the back into a collar of yellow which spreads onto the breast. The throat beneath the black mask is tinged with orange. Their bellies are light green, wings are dark green, rumps are green with a faint violet blue wash on the lower part and on the upper tail coverts; tails are green, marked with orange yellow and black. The irides are brown and the bare eye rings are, of course, white.

Breeding
As long as their aviary is in a sheltered position and they have a box in which to roost; they are able to withstand winter weather in Britain, and in fact they will breed through the winter. Cooler, damp weather seems to be an incentive to breeding which generally declines in the summer heat.

Willow branches and twigs are the favourite home building materials; the birds will strip the willow into small pieces and weave it into a cosy enclosed nest within the box. They will soak odd pieces of willow in their water dish, either to make it supple enough to work, or possibly to keep humidity in the nest at the correct level required to prevent chicks being dead-in-shell and promote good hatchability.

The nesting material is carried in the bird's bill. The nest is made in such a way that, to inspect the eggs or young, it is generally necessary to tear or remove part of it which results in the parents deserting. It is best to stifle curiosity and leave well alone.

Two to five young are usually raised in a nest; they differ in appearance from the adults in having dark marks at the base of the bill, (young Blue Maskeds have yellowish bills and Blue hatchlings have white down instead of orange). They have dark nails and black freckles on their feet; these black freckles stay for quite a long time, even into the first moult. Plumage colour is the same as the adults but less brilliant.

Food
Feeding should be the same as mentioned for the other species, except that the Masked always ignore apple, but they do enjoy a little

brown bread moistened with water or with milk. A multivitamin solution or vitamin and mineral powder can be added to this. Soaked millet spray is a great favourite and can be quickly soaked and softened with boiling water; extra spray should be given when there are young in the nest.

Most lovebirds eat a lot of cuttlefish bone and the Masked are no exception. They should never be deprived of this material otherwise eggbinding through soft shelled eggs will result

When the young are weaned it is best not to put two or more nests of young in the same cage or flight as fighting between the families may ensue even at this young age.

Sexing is difficult as individual strains show varying characteristics in appearance between cocks and hens. However, generally speaking, hens have wider, flatter bellies while cocks are slimmer and longer in the body. There *seems* at the time of writing to be a predominance of hens bred, especially with the Blue Masked; the balance of the sexes is usually about even I have found.

Colour Mutations

Adding to the general interest of this species are the three well-known colour mutations, Blue, Yellow (Dilute) and White (Dilute Blue). The latter being produced by combining the factors of the previous two.

In 1927 a Blue Masked caught wild was imported into Britain from Tanzania (then Tanganyika) strangely enough only a short period after the first normal Masked were imported. This first Blue went to the London Zoo and was subsequently found to be a cock.

David Seth-Smith, F.Z.S., during his office as editor of the *Avicultural Magazine* gave the origins and description of this bird in the issue of February 1928. This article was accompanied by a fine full colour plate from an original by the artist Roland Green. The painting was commissioned by a Mr Chapman, an often-mentioned importer and procurer of rare specimens and, in fact, the original importer of the bird in question.

Several Californian aviculturists in the early 1930s were most surprised to discover young blues among the progeny of Masked lovebirds which were thought to be normals. The Californian climate was ideal for the Blue Maskeds so they thrived and multiplied and continue to do so to this day. After the Second World War when stocks of aviary birds in Europe were decimated, aviaries in Britain and other European countries were replenished with these Californian Blues.

The Japanese were also breeding the Blue Masked and it was not long before there was such a surplus in Japan that Blues were cheaper than Normals; this led to the glut being exported to Europe where they did not, unfortunately, prove to be such a success as those from the USA.

After many years of struggle the Blue Masked was firmly established in Britain. Even so, most people used to over coddle them and not only keep them in through the winter but try to breed them inside all the year round which, apart from poor breeding results occurring, only continued in keeping them soft.

(The author decided to build a hardy outdoor strain which was done with three original birds. A breeding stock of thirty to forty birds, the produce of this meagre beginning, was maintained for several years, until it was decided to change over to mutations of Peach-Faced.)

In Britain, Mr John Wood of Cheltenham imports large numbers of lovebirds. In a recent consignment of three thousand Masked lovebirds caught wild, and imported from Tanzania, there was one lone blue specimen. This bird is the same in appearance as those bred in Britain.

The Blue Masked is a true blue mutation; yellow areas are changed to white, green areas to pure blue, the black head remains the same but the violet blue rump is more conspicuous than in the normal. The bill is changed from red to pale pink. (Incidentally, it has always been a puzzle to me why the bill of the Blue mutant Indian Ringneck Parrakeet *Psittacula krameri manillensis* should have a red bill like the Normal for this too is a true blue mutant as is proved by the pink collar being changed to white.)

The Yellow Masked has been established for quite some time. The yellow areas remain the same, green areas are mottled yellow/green, the head is brown and the bill remains red. This mutation said to have originated in Japan, is really a dilute and recessive. This Dilute factor was combined with the Blue factor to produce the White (or Dilute Blue) and all three colours have been exported to Britain from Japan at various times.

The White Masked is possibly the least interesting in appearance being merely a washed out Blue. It is not a separate mutation but, as has been said, a combination of the Blue and the Yellow (Dilute) factors.

There have been offered for sale birds known as Greys supposedly originating from Japan. As the none-too-common Cinnamon was said to have originated in Japan, these so-called Greys could have

56

been the result of combining the Cinnamon factor with the Blue. It should also be possible to combine the Dilute factor with the Cinnamon and the Blue and this might produce birds of a paler and more even colour, i.e., Dilute Cinnamon Normals and Dilute Cinnamon Blues. This Cinnamon factor in Maskeds is said to be sex-linked and the breeding pattern would be:

Pairing
Cinnamon cock × Cinnamon hen ⟶

Colour of Young
Cinnamon cocks and hens

Cinnamon cock × Normal hen ⟶ Cinnamon hens and Normal cocks/Cinnamon

Normal cock × Cinnamon hen ⟶ Normal hens and Normal cocks/Cinnamon

Normal cock/Cinnamon
  × Normal hen ⟶ Normal hens, Cinnamon hens, Normal cocks and Normal cocks/Cinnamon

Normal cock/Cinnamon
  × Cinnamon hen ⟶ Cinnamon cocks and hens, Normal hens and Normal cocks/Cinnamon

To breed Cinnamon Blues:

Pairing
1 Cinnamon cock × Blue hen ⟶

Colour of Young
Cinnamon hens/Blue and Normal cocks/Cinnamon and Blue

2 **Normal cock/Cinnamon and Blue** × Blue hen ⟶ Normal hens/Blue, Cinnamon hens/Blue, Normal cocks/Blue, Normal cocks/Blue and Cinnamon, Blue hens, **Cinnamon Blue hens**, Blue cocks and Blue cocks/Cinnamon

or:

2 **Normal cock/Cinnamon and Blue × Cinnamon hen/Blue** ⟶ Cinnamon cocks and hens, Normal hens, Normal cocks/Cinnamon, Cinnamon cocks/Blue, Cinnamon hens/Blue, Normal hens/Blue, Normal cocks/Cinnamon and Blue, **Cinnamon Blue hens, Cinnamon Blue cocks**, Blue hens and Blue cocks/Cinnamon

To illustrate how to breed Cinnamon Yellows (Cinnamon Dilutes) simply replace 'Blue' and 'Yellow' (Dilute) in the above formulas.

To breed Cinnamon Whites (Cinnamon Dilute Blues) one method would be:

57

Pairing	Colour of Young
1 Cinnamon Normal cock × White hen ⟶	**Normal cocks/Blue, Yellow, White and Cinnamon** and Cinnamon Normal hens/Blue, Yellow and White
2 **Normal cock/Blue, Yellow, White and Cinnamon** × White hen ⟶	Cocks and hens Normals/White, Blues/White, Yellows/White and Whites and Normal cocks/Cinnamon White, Blue cocks/Cinnamon White, Yellow cocks/Cinnamon White and White cocks/Cinnamon and Cinnamon normal hens/White, Cinnamon Blue hens/White, Cinnamon Yellow hens/White and **Cinnamon White hens**

There are Pied Masked lovebirds, although the ones seen hardly seem to merit the name, the variegation having been limited to a few yellow flights in the normals and white flights in the Blues. I do not know of any established strain and therefore can give no information on their genetics.

The most recent development with Maskeds is that of recessive Lutinos and Albinos. These have taken eight years to develop from a cross between a Lutino Fischer's (recessive) and White Masked (recessive – Dilute Blue). This achievement is the work of the well-known Dutch aviculturist Mr J. J. Postema.

The Albino masked which has been produced is completely snow white with red eyes, pink feet and bill; the Lutino is golden yellow with white flights, red eyes, pink feet, red bill and retains a pinkish red head.

In the following list of expectations of the most common Masked mutations none of the colours (Normal, Blue, Yellow and White) are sex-linked. It therefore has no bearing on the resulting colours of the young whether the father or mother carries the factor or factors for the mutation(s). For example:

Pairing	Colour of Young
Normal cock × Blue hen ⟶	All young are Normals/Blue
Blue cock × Normal hen ⟶	All young are Normals/Blue

58

Breeding Pattern for the Colour Mutations of the Masked Lovebird:

Pairing	Colour of Young
Normal × Normal ⟶	All Normals
Normal × Blue ⟶	All Normals/Blue
Normal/Blue × Normal/Blue ⟶	Normals, Normals/Blue and Blues
Normal/Blue × Blue ⟶	Normals/Blue and Blues
Normal/Blue × Normal ⟶	Normals and Normals/Blue
Blue × Blue ⟶	All Blues
Normal × Yellow ⟶	All Normals/Yellow
Normal/Yellow × Normal/Yellow ⟶	Normals, Normals/Yellow and Yellows
Normal/Yellow × Yellow ⟶	Normals/Yellow and Yellows
Normal/Yellow × Normal ⟶	Normals and Normals/Yellow
Yellow × Yellow ⟶	All Yellows

Blue and Yellow factors

The combination of the Blue and Yellow factors shows a more complicated pattern:

Pairing	Colour of Young
Yellow × Blue ⟶	Normals/Blue, Yellow and White
Normal × Normal/Blue, Yellow and White ⟶	Normals and Normals/Blue, Yellow and White
Normal/Blue, Yellow and White × Normal/Blue ⟶	Normals, Normals/Blue, Normals/Yellow, Normals/White, Blues and Blues/White
Normal/Blue, Yellow and White × Normal/Yellow ⟶	Normals, Normals/Blue, Normals/Yellow, Normals/White, Yellows and Yellows/White
Normal/Blue, Yellow and White × Normal/Blue, Yellow and White ⟶	Normals, Blues, Yellows, Whites, Normals/White, Normals/Blue, Normals/Yellow, Blues/White, Yellows/White and Normals/White
Normal/Blue, Yellow and White × Blue ⟶	Normals/Blue, Normals/White, Blues and Blues/White
Normal/Blue, Yellow and White × Yellow ⟶	Normals/Yellow, Normals/White, Yellows and Yellows/White

59

Normal/Blue, Yellow and
   White × White ────────────→ Normals/White, Blues/White,
                                           Yellows/White and Whites

Normal/Blue × Normal/Yellow ──→ Normals, Normals/Blue,
                                           Normals/Yellow and Normals/White

White × Blue ────────────────→ All Blues/White

White × Blue/White ──────────→ Blues/White and Whites

White × Yellow ──────────────→ All Yellows/White

White × Yellow/White ────────→ Yellows/White and Whites

White × White ───────────────→ All Whites

Peach-Faced Lovebird *Agapornis roseicollis roseicollis*
Size 15 cm (5·9 in)

The Peach-Faced Lovebird inhabits a vast area of arid coastal plain and savannah including the whole of Namibia, extending to the Cape Province and Botswana, and in the north to Angola. The latter area, the southern part of Angola, is inhabited by the sub-species *Agapornis roseicollis catumbella* which differs from the nominate race in having the head and face of a deeper red and a deeper pink, the body and wings are a more brilliant green and the rump is a deeper blue.

The Peach-Faced are plentiful in their range and make themselves conspicuous with their activities and noisy chatter. Their food consists of the seeding grasses and so on which are to be found in their habitat plus watever they can steal from ripening crops. They invade the large communal nests of the resident species of Weaver birds, allowing their hosts to use the sections they do not need.

First discovered in 1793, the Peach-Faced were considered to be the same species as Red-Faced for twenty-four years, after which it was admitted that they were a separate species. Imported into Britain for the first time in the early 1860s, and, considering their prolifacy nowadays, if they were given any encouragement at all breeding successes must have followed swiftly.

Like most of the other lovebirds, the Peach-Faced are darker green above and lighter green below; rumps are bright blue but the shade of blue is variable, foreheads are pinkish red and face, throat and upper breast are pink. The tail is green, marked with dull red and black, the irides are very dark brown and the bill is pale flesh-coloured with the tip and edges tinged with a pale green, as if stained with the juice of plants they had been eating.

The Peach-Faced must be the most widely bred and highly domesticated of the genus because of its readiness to nest.

Peach-faced chicks.

Breeding

If allowed to do so, they will breed anytime of the year in outside flights and will tolerate regular nest inspection.

They are very difficult to sex, but there are a few pointers. Receptive partners in breeding condition will reveal their gender by the cock's act of regurgitating food and the hen's accepting it. Only rarely will one cock feed another. The hen doesn't call for food but begs for it by looking round into the cock's face and bobbing her head.

If a pair continually bicker or show no signs of nesting over a long period, it is best to split them up and give them new partners (they are most likely of the same sex). Sometimes birds are just totally incompatible.

The pelvic bone test is inconsistent as the pelvic bones of hens out of breeding condition can be closed up tight while some adult breeding cocks have been found to have pelvic bones as wide apart as young hens coming into breeding condition. Of course, laying hens have the pelvic bones very wide apart to allow the eggs to be passed,

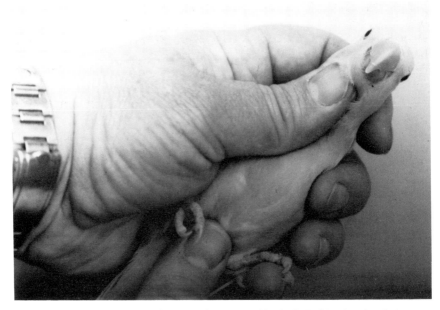

The distance between the pelvic bones can be measured by the ball of the thumb or index finger.

but by this time the sex of the bird is obvious without examining the pelvic bones. Breeder hens have wider, flatter bellies than cocks but this is not evident in young birds to any marked degree.

It is not true that only hens carry nesting material (which they do by tucking it under their rump feathers), as some of our breeding cocks will carry material into the nest in the same manner as the hens. Cocks will roost on top of a box, in a food cup or on a high perch besides sleeping inside a nest box; hens will rarely roost out if there is a nestbox to hand.

Cock's heads are generally fractionally bolder and brighter than are the hens; also the cocks are a slightly sharper, acid green than hens. But, just to confuse things, there are hens which are larger and brighter than normal, and cocks which are smaller and duller than normal. Apart from differences in individual strains, there are the differences between the specimens from the nominate race and the sub-species and the combinations between them to be considered.

The method of sexing by comparing the birds' tails, whether they are held slightly fanned or closed and narrow, is also inconsistent I have found. The theory is that the usually dominant partner, the hen, displays her dominance by holding her tail fanned while the henpecked partner, the cock, shows his subservience to the hen by holding his tail closed and narrow. But, once again, things are not always so black and white as some cocks dominate their hens. Also, hens which are shown obviously to be hens by the fact that they are full of eggs tend to fan their tails in any case because of the bulk and width of their lower abdomen at this time. In all there is no single factor that points definitely to the sex of a bird and the only proof of a true pair is fertile eggs.

Nestboxes can be made of 12 mm to 25 mm plywood (half to one inch). A convenient size is 150 mm × 180 mm × 250 mm high (6 in × 7 in × 10 in) with a removable lid and entrance hole right at the top; they are hung at head height under cover.

Willow is the perfect material for nest making and should be fixed high up in the flight to draw the attention of the birds. If a few twigs of willow are given each day this maintains the interest in nest building, and stimulates the birds into breeding conditions. Most of the leaves are removed before the willow is given to them. (It may be coincidence but we have found a high number of crop and digestive troubles when a surfeit of willow leaves have been available to the

A simple type of nestbox which has proved satisfactory for the Peach-Faced and Eye-ringed species. (Do not make a door in the side as the birds will try to fill the cracks with building material which will fall back on eggs or young when the door is opened.)

birds.) The nest is cup shaped and has no dome.

Should the hen be full of eggs, about to lay and yet the nest is still not made, then some dried grass (not hay, which may contain spores of harmful moulds) or used millet sprays should be stripped up and rammed into the bottom of the box to make a bed for the eggs. Take care not to use those sprays which have been on the flight floor because they may be full of mite.

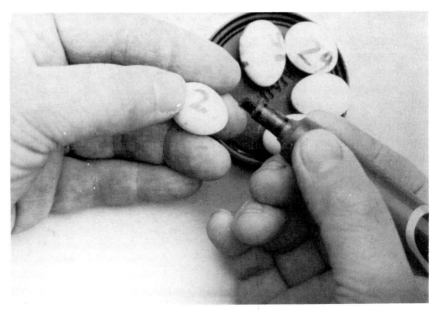

Numbering eggs with a spirit marker.

As the eggs are laid it is useful to mark them with the date and the number of the flight with a felt tip spirit marker. These marks stay on until the eggs hatch and are very useful for identification purposes should it be needed to foster them out.

Ringing

I do not like to ring my young birds, as so many accidents and problems can be caused with rings. Chicks that have been rung have been mutilated; adult birds have had severed tendons and lost feet when the ring has hooked onto a piece of wire; the bird has nibbled the ring until it has a sharp edge or it has been squashed up tight into the bird's leg. I usually remove rings as soon as possible using them for identification for short periods only.

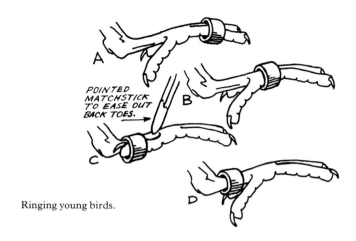

POINTED
MATCHSTICK
TO EASE OUT
BACK TOES. →

Ringing young birds.

However, if you wish to ring young birds with closed rings it is quite simple to do, having obtained the correct size and ascertained that the metal will withstand the pressure of the birds' bills. The front toes are pushed through the ring, the ring eased over the ball of the foot and the two hind toes eased out with a pointed matchstick. The ring can be covered with the birds' excreta to prevent it being drawn to the attention of the parent birds who may try to remove it. The exact age at which the ring will slip over and behind the toes without working back off again must be judged by trial and error. This is usually between a week and ten days.

Food
With regard to feeding, I give mainly 50/50 canary and white millet with liberal amounts of panicum and Japanese millet plus a small amount of sunflower. Apple sprinkled with a little vitamin and mineral powder (SA37 made by Intervet) is given every day. A little hard or boiled whole maize is also appreciated. Seeding grass and chickweed is given when available. There are many other types of wildfood which are enjoyed, dandilion heads, shepherd's purse and sow thistle among them. They do not seem to like elder and hawthorn berries which Parrakeets relish. Cuttlefish bone is available at all times. The flights are gravelled and so the birds pick this over for grit, but a good mineralised grit would be beneficial. To encourage breeding, and when young hatch, soaked millet spray and moistened brown bread is given.

Care must be taken to see that the water receptacles are cleaned every day as the Peach-Faced are rather prone to sour crop which is a problem when water dishes are on the ground, particularly in warm weather. They will not only soak nesting material in the dishes but will put in large stones, lumps of dirt and seed. This makes the water go sour in a very short time. We find it best to use large cups which are hooked onto the wire of the flight at about head height.

Characteristics
When the young are weaned they will sometimes tolerate sharing their flight with another brood of weaners. But care should be taken, even though domesticated lovebirds are nothing like as spiteful with one another as were their wild ancestors. It is adviseable to house only one breeding pair to a flight, especially if the aviary is small. This is necessary if serious colour breeding is being pursued otherwise the exact parentage of the young cannot be established without doubt.

Normal young differ from their parents in having most of the red and pink areas of the head a greenish grey; most of the upper mandible, and sometimes the lower, are dark brown from the base. The rest of the plumage is generally duller than in adults. They start to attain their adult coloration after only a few weeks out of the nest.

Eggs are laid every other day, usually a clutch of four to six which take twenty-two days to hatch, incubation starting from about the second or third egg.

The Peach-Faced are mature enough to breed at four months old though some individuals show no interest in nesting until well over a year old. It is best to try to hold them back till they are about a year old. The breeding pair will go to nest again between two weeks and a month after the young fledge. In general it is advisable to take three nests and then give the birds a rest. Up to seven, but generally four or five are reared in one nest.

If it is wished to rest breeding pairs which have proved too prolific breeding can be discouraged in several ways. The first and most obvious way is to split up the pairs into couples or groups of the same sex housed together, if they will agree. Nestboxes and nesting materials should be removed which means that birds which usually roost in nestboxes risk being chilled in wintry weather, in this case it is advisable to keep them in flight cages in an unheated shed. Removing all nesting material and giving them no more fresh willow will discourage them to some extent but if really keen they will whittle the framework of the aviary for their purposes and carry on regardless.

Another method is to move the pairs around into different flights periodically so that the surroundings are unfamiliar, this distracts them and puts them off breeding for a while.

If the hen is already full of eggs she must be allowed to lay the clutch. The eggs can be dipped in boiling water for long enough to kill the germ in the egg and then given back to the hen to incubate. While the hen is sitting the pair are having quite a restful time. It is the production of the eggs and the feeding of the young for six or more weeks that drains the strength from the pair.

The Peach-Faced very often come into breeding condition in the late summer (in Britain) and breed through autumn and into early winter. If possible, it is best to encourage breeding through the spring and summer months when the young will have warmer weather and longer days which will make them grow more quickly. The young can be heard in the nest calling for food throughout the night so the parents must fill their crops sufficiently to sustain their young and themselves till morning.

Our dimensions for breeding flights are 610 cm wide, 122 cm long and 183 cm high (2 ft × 4 ft × 6 ft) with cover at each end. The front is filled in up to waist height with plastic sheeting but the shelters are not enclosed. The wire partitions between each flight are not double wired and though occasionally a toe gets nipped no serious damage is done between one neighbour and another.

I have been equally successful with smaller flights measuring three feet (915 mm) long by sixteen inches (410 mm) wide and three feet (915 mm) high with wire mesh floors and standing three feet off the ground.

Mutation Colours of the Peach-Faced

Of all the species of lovebirds the Peach-Faced has the highest number of mutant colour forms occurring. As it is also the hardiest and easiest bred, it is predicted that in a few years its popularity will have grown to such an extent as to merit its own specialist society which will lead to standards of excellence being laid down for exhibition purposes.

The mutant colour factors which have so far appeared are Pied, Pastel Blue, Dilute (in at least two depths), Lutino, Olive (Dark factor), Cinnamon and now there are reports of pure White Faced Blues. When these factors are combined in various permutations a whole galaxy of new colour varieties can be produced. It will take several years to explore all the possibilities these existing factors offer during which time some more new and interesting ones may have arisen.

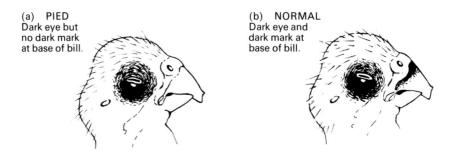

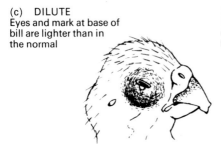

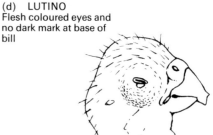

(a) PIED
Dark eye but
no dark mark
at base of bill.

(b) NORMAL
Dark eye and
dark mark at
base of bill.

(c) DILUTE
Eyes and mark at base of
bill are lighter than in
the normal

(d) LUTINO
Flesh coloured eyes and
no dark mark at base of
bill

Predicting the colour variety of Peach-Faced hatchlings by examining their eyes and bills.

N.B. The primary down of hatchling Pastel Blues, Pied Pastel Blues, Dilute Pastel Blues (Silver Cherries), Cream Lutinos and all those combining the Pastel Blue factor visually with several other factors is always *white*. The primary down of hatchlings lacking the Pastel Blue Factor (i.e. Normals, Pied Normals, Dilute Normals (Golden Cherry), Lutinos, Olives and their combinations) is pinkish orange.

Care must be taken also to study the differences in brilliance of colour, sparkle and luminosity, quality of feather, darkness and lightness of colour, matt feather texture, well balanced size and proportion of entire physical shape, and so on; subtle differences and qualities in individual specimens which the breeder can employ to improve his stock and make differences in colour more striking and diverse.

Pieds

The pied factor is dominant and visually extremely variable. (This mutation is said to have first appeared in California in the mid 1930s.) It can be present in a bird merely as a small patch of yellow on the head, as a single white flight, a white nail or patch of pink flesh on the

68

feet, or can be up to 100% variegated. Birds may also be affected by having the remaining green areas diluted to a patchy green.

A good marked Pied should be heavily marked with golden yellow on head, breast and wings with clear white flights. The green areas should be as dark as in the normal to provide a good foil and contrast with the yellow. The rump should remain deep blue and looks most attractive when framed between the white flight feathers. The area and depth of colour of the red and pink on the face can also be lessened by the Pied factor.

It should be possible, with continued selective breeding, to develop strains with a particular and precise pattern of variegation which will breed true to form (for example, a green bird with all yellow head and wings). This was done with the Australian Banded Pied Budgerigar which has a light patch on the back of the head, light flights and tail and a light belt or band across the belly.

Birds of high variegation tend to produce a higher percentage of highly variegated young than do lesser variegated birds especially when paired to partners like themselves, also a higher percentage of pied young. But birds of lesser variegation can also produce highly variegated young, though fewer of them.

The yellow on the hen birds is not as golden as the yellow areas on the cocks. Hatchling Pieds, even those with quite a small area of variegation when grown, can be detected in the nest by examining their bills which will have no dark colour at their bases as do hatchling normals. The young Pieds' bills will stay yellow, or yellow with a few dark streaks from the base, until they begin to mature.

The secondary down of the young Pieds is creamy white while that of the Normals is grey; again this is true even for those lovebirds with comparatively little variegation in their plumage.

The light areas in the plumage of the Pied will improve in colour and increase in size until the bird attains the age of two years. In some individuals the dark areas will deepen, have added sparkle and contrast more strongly with the pied areas, while in some they will lighten and perhaps become more matt.

It seems that the pied factor can be concentrated genetically; that is if Pied is paired to Pied continually for generation after generation not only is the overall quality and variegation improved but the Pieds' ability to reproduce their own variety is increased and they become more dominant genetically, so much so that when one of these concentrated Pieds is paired to a Normal the progeny are all pied to some extent, whereas a Pied bred from Pied crossed with a Normal will produce a certain amount of Normals as well as Pieds. For the purpose of simplification we will call them *Single Pieds* (single factor Pieds) and *Double Pieds* (double factor Pieds).

Pairing	Colour of Young
Single Pied × Normal ⟶	Single Pieds and Normals
Single Pied × Single Pied ⟶	Double Pieds, Single Pieds and Normals
Double Pied × Normal ⟶	All Single Pieds
Double Pied × Single Pied ⟶	Double Pieds and Single Pieds
Double Pied × Double Pied ⟶	All Double Pieds

Recessive Pied Peach-Faced lovebirds probably exist but they are difficult to trace, therefore it must be assumed that all those which are commonly available in Britain are of the Dominant type in which case it is difficult to see how a Normal can be split for Pied. Having mated Normals bred from Pieds for several seasons and not having produced any Pieds whatever from these matings, the conclusion is that the normal-looking birds which are bred from Pieds mask no Pied factor and cannot be split for Pied. When told by breeders (generally novices) that they have bred Pieds from Normals split for Pied, further enquiry has proved that one or both of the parents are very slightly Pied visually. Some breeders call these slightly Pied birds split Pieds; in fact birds with quite a minute amount of variegation (just a 'tick') can transmit the Pied factor to their young, and these may show a much higher percentage of variegation than their parents. The Pied mark may not even be in the plumage but perhaps on a foot or toe where the skin will be pink instead of grey.

There are one or two other interesting points to be noted regarding Pieds. Normal-looking birds which have been bred from Pieds produce Pieds of better quality with slightly more Pied young when they are mated to Pieds than do normal-looking birds having no Pied ancestry. Also, in rare cases, a normal-looking bird which has been bred from Pieds will moult out into a visual pied when it matures and produce Pied young itself. This can happen when the bird is so advanced as to be in its second year. These birds are able to pass on the visual pied factor to their young.

In the early 1950s Mr Parker and Mr Braine in South Africa developed a strain of Yellow Peach-Faced lovebirds by inbreeding with a slightly pied hen which had moulted out clear yellow. These birds retained the pink head but lost the blue rump. The most interesting fact with this strain was that the young always left the nest in green plumage and moulted out into Yellows as they attained their adult plumage. From this inbred line several all red (Red Suffused) birds were also produced.

Yellows derived from Pieds
Yellows have been developed by selectively breeding from Pieds of high variegation until 90% to 100% of the green areas are changed to yellow. The yellow colour varies in intensity from lemon to golden yellow. Cocks are slightly deeper yellow than hens.

A perfect Yellow should have a deep pink face and throat, golden yellow abdomen and wings, white flights, yellow and pink tail; it should retain the bright blue rump.

Green flecks are undesirable, none the less a bird showing no foul markings would be quite rare and as can be imagined production of these Yellows takes a great deal of patience and can prove to be frustrating to the breeder.

Pastel Blue
The Pastel Blue Peach-Faced occurred in the aviaries of Mr P. Habets of Holland in 1963. They were brought to Britain in the early 1970's and have been so prolific that in a few short years they have become the most commonly offered and cheapest of all mutant lovebirds.

Though Pastel Blues are a very beautiful addition to our aviaries, it must be made clear that they are not a true blue mutation like the Blue Masked or Blue Indian Ringneck Parrakeet but go only half way. Perhaps a better name could have been given to them, such as 'Sea Blue' or 'Semi-Blue' which would be more descriptive. However they have become universally known as Pastel Blues and this name does serve to distinguish them from true Blues.

A true Blue would have a white face, there should be no hint of pink at all. Similarly, when a true Blue is combined with pied or lutino factors the areas of plumage which are yellow in Pieds and Lutinos are changed to white. However, if the pastel blue factor is combined with the other two factors these areas are a cream or buttermilk colour.

Pastel Blues are similar, in colour and genetically, to the Blue Splendid Grass Parrakeet *Neophema splendida*; the apricot pink colour of its breast is identical to the colour of the forehead of the Pastel Blue. Both birds also show a slight variation in the colour of the blue areas (i.e. those areas which are green in the Normal birds) which vary from sea-green to blue with a turquoise tinge.

The Pastel Blue is mainly turquoise blue to sea blue, darker above, lighter below. The throat is ivory with a slight blush of pink, forehead apricot pink, rump brilliant cobalt blue and bills and eyes are the same as in the Normals. They are recessive, and the breeding pattern is as follows:

Pairing	Colour of Young
Pastel Blue × Normal ⟶	All Normals/Pastel Blue
Pastel Blue × Normal/Pastel Blue ⟶	Normals/Pastel Blue and Pastel Blues
Normal/Pastel Blue × Normal/Pastel Blue ⟶	Normals, Normals/Pastel Blue and Pastel Blues
Normal/Pastel Blue × Normal ⟶	Normals and Normals/Pastel Blue
Pastel Blue × Pastel Blue ⟶	All Pastel Blues

Hatchling Pastel Blues can be detected in a nest of mixed colours by their primary down which is white. With Pastel Blues the depth of colour of the plumage can be an indicator of sex. Cocks are generally a slightly greener shade of blue than hens, also the colour of their foreheads is brighter.

Pied Pastel Blues

The Pied Pastel Blue is obtained quite simply by combining, as would be expected, the Pied factor with the Pastel Blue factor, as follows:

Pairing	Colour of Young
1 Single Pied Normal × Pastel Blue ⟶	Normals/Pastel Blue and **Single Pied Normals/Pastel Blue**
2 **Single Pied Normal/Pastel Blue** × Pastel Blue ⟶	Normals/Pastel Blue, Pastel Blues, Single Pied Normals/Pastel Blue and **Single Pied Pastel Blues**

and so on:

3 **Single Pied Pastel Blue × Single Pied Pastel Blue** ⟶	Pastel Blues, **Single Pied Pastel Blues** and **Double Pied Pastel Blues**

Hatchling Pied Pastel Blues can be detected in the nest by their primary down being white and by the lack of dark colour at the base of the bill. The secondary down of youngsters is creamy white instead of grey as with ordinary Pastel Blues.

The Pied areas of the plumage are a creamy buttermilk colour which becomes more yellowish above as the bird matures. Adult Pied Pastel Blues of high variegation have a much more orange forehead.

Buttermilk derived from Pied Pastel Blues
The Buttermilk (the most suitable name to describe the rich creamy plumage) is the ultimate product of selective breeding of Pied Pastel Blues with a high percentage of variegation, a parallel with the Yellow derived from Pieds.

The ideal specimen would be buttermilk (cream) in body colour, richer on the wings, have white flights, a pale orange forehead, pale ivory throat with a blush of pink and bright blue rump for contrast.

Hatchling Buttermilks are the same in appearance as Pied Pastel Blues.

Dilute (Golden Cherry)
There appear to be three separate mutants of the Dilute Peach-Faced, commonly known as the Golden Cherry Peach-Faced. The originator of one type, Mr Masaru Iwata of Nagoya, Japan, named his mutant the Japanese Imperial Golden Cherryhead Lovebird, in the early 1950s.

The European breeders refer to the darker type as Golden Cherry, or American Golden Cherry, and the paler type as Golden Yellow, or Japanese Golden Cherry. Although it is not clear if these types have been credited with their correct origins, as there are both light and dark types established in Europe, USA, probably Japan (at least one type) and Australia, it will probably be simpler to name them after the reported countries of origin.

The pale type of Dilute mutation which has been established in Australia originated in the aviaries of Mr Ron Fisk of Sydney. These birds are canary yellow with a pale blue rump, white flights, dark eyes and are recessive to normal. It would be convenient if these were to be called Australian Dilutes.

A further suggestion is that the pale type of Dilute to be found in Europe, known as the Japanese Golden Cherry, should be known as the Japanese Dilute even though it is possible that they originally came from Australia via the USA. If it is eventually found that the Australian and Japanese Dilutes are the same in origin (and therefore the same genetically) then one name must be decided on.

The Japanese Dilutes are the same in appearance as the Australian Dilute, both have a faint lime iridescent suffusion. When crossed with the dark type of Dilute, which it is suggested be known as the American Dilute, Normal looking birds (which should be split for both Japanese and American Dilute) are produced I am informed; this is proof that the two are completely separate mutations.

Although a dark type of Dilute is established in Australia which is

73

identical genetically and in appearance to the American Dilute (from which it is possible the Americans originated their dark type Dilutes by initially importing them) it is difficult to ascertain what results are obtained when these are crossed with the Australian (pale) Dilutes. This information would help considerably in formulating the genetic alliances between the various types.

As the dark type Dilute of Australia is most probably the same as the American Dilute (unless identical mutations did occur in both countries) it is suggested that the name American Dilute be used as the one name to describe the dark type in order to prevent confusion between it and the Australian Dilute of the pale type.

To summarise, the three mutants of Dilute Golden Cherry are:

1 The Australian Dilute (pale type which may be one and the same as No. 2).
2 The Japanese Dilute
3 The American Dilute (dark type)

Of all the Dilutes, the American is of most interest to the author because of its elusive and altering colour.

This mutation affects the appearance of the Peach-Faced in several ways. The green of the Normal is replaced by a lime gold colour which of all the mutant colours is the one most altered by the varying light of day; in subdued light or in shade it appears to be a dull lime colour while in brilliant sunlight it is a rich gold, not yellow. (This is illustrated by the colour illustrations of this mutant which are shown both in light and shade.) The face, throat and forehead remain the same colour as in the Normal but more extensive, the rump is streaked with a pale iridescent blue, the flights are pale grey with a dark quill and dark pencilling around the edges; the larger wing coverts are likewise quilled and pencilled as is the tail which is also marked with grey and brick red.

Hatchling American Dilutes have plum coloured eyes which, unfortunately, soon darken. The youngsters' bills are not marked with dark brown like Normals but with a paler brown; also they lack the golden hue of the adults being, in all lights, a dull lime colour. The secondary down of the young is much paler than that of Normals.

The three types of Dilute are all recessive to Normal:

Pairing	Colour of Young
Australian Dilute × Normal ⟶	All Normals/Australian Dilute
Japanese Dilute × Normal ⟶	All Normals/Japanese Dilute
American Dilute × Normal ⟶	All Normals/American Dilute
Japanese Dilute × American Dilute ⟶	All Normals/? American and Japanese Dilute?

N.B. To obtain the full formula insert 'Dilute' instead of 'Pastel Blue' in the previously given formula for Pastel Blue.

Dilute Pastel Blue (Silver Cherry)
The Dilute Pastel Blue, commonly known as the Silver Cherry, is produced by combining the American Dilute factor with the Pastel Blue. The golden or lime colour of the American Dilute is replaced by a pale grey with a slight greenish cast, the forehead is apricot pink, throat ivory with a pink blush and the flights, tail and wing coverts are marked in the same way as the American Dilutes; the tail lacks the red barring.

Due to the Pastel Blue factor, the down of the hatchlings is white; eyes of hatchlings are plum coloured due to the Dilute factor.

If the Pastel Blue factor is combined with the Japanese or Australian Dilute factor, the resulting young will be a cream colour rather than pale grey.

The pairings to produce Dilute Pastel Blues are as follows:

Pairing	Colour of Young
1 Dilute × Pastel Blue ⟶	**All Normals/Pastel Blue and Dilute**
2 **Normal/Pastel Blue and Dilute × Normal/Pastel Blue and Dilute** ⟶	Normals, Normals/Dilute, Normals/Pastel Blue, Normals/Pastel Blue and Dilute, Pastel Blues, Pastel Blue/Dilute, Dilutes, Dilutes/Blue and **Dilute Pastel Blues**

Pied Dilutes
To combine the Pied factor with the Japanese Dilute or the Australian Dilute would be pointless as the pied markings would be hardly noticeable against the already yellow body. But combined with the darker American Dilute and the American Dilute Pastel Blue (Pied Golden Cherry and Pied Silver Cherry) some interesting and subtle Pastel colour variations are created:

Pairing	Colour of Young
1 Single Pied Normal × American Dilute ⟶	**Single Pied Normals/American Dilute** and Normals/American Dilute
2 **Single Pied Normal/American Dilute × American Dilute** ⟶	Single Pied Normals/American Dilute, Normals/American Dilute, American Dilutes and **Single Pied American Dilutes**

Thirdly, to produce Pied Dilute Pastel Blues use the same method of pairings substituting Pied Pastel Blue for Pied Normal and American Dilute Pastel Blue for American Dilute.

Olive (Double Dark Factor)

The Olive originated in the avairies of Mr Allan Hollingsworth of Ivanhoe, Victoria, Australia. It has been in existence for some years in Australia and is now well established. It is to me the most interesting of the mutant factors and enables the breeder to produce all the foregoing colours and combinations in three tones, light (Normal) Single Dark factor and Double Dark factor.

In appearance the Olive (Double Dark factor Green) is khaki or brownish-green where the Normal is pale green (lighter below, darker above); the pink on forehead, face and throat is the same as in the Normal, the rump is most striking being a slate grey with a slight mauvish tinge, the flights are almost black and so is the tail, but with carmine pink markings. The young have very dark, almost black, bases to their bills.

The dark factor works exactly the same with Peach-Faced as it does with Budgerigars and seems to have only occured in these two species of Psittacine birds.

The Jade (Single Dark factor Green) is produced when the Olive is paired to a Light Green (Normal) and differs quite noticeably from the Light Green in being a laurel green in body colour with a darker blue rump.

Care must be taken to use this mutant to produce specific mutant combinations and not to use it haphazardly or strains of useful extra-brilliantly coloured Peach-Faced could be dulled and spoilt.

Some fallacies which have arisen about the potentialities of the Dark factor (Olive) should be corrected. Firstly, using the Dark factor in combination with the Pastel Blue factor will not create a true cobalt coloured bird, just a darker Pastel Blue (Single Dark factor Pastel Blue). Likewise combining the Dark factor with the Pastel Blue and Lutino factors does not produce a pure white Albino nor even a whiter Cream Lutino. The Dark factor is overlaid on existing colours, it does not make them disappear. Those areas which are visually red, pink, yellow or cream in the bird before the Dark factor is added will not be altered by it one fraction.

The Dark factor works as follows:

Pairing	Colour of Young
Olive (Double Dark factor) × Light Green (Normal) ⟶	All Jades (Single Dark factor)

76

Jade × Light Green ─────────────→ Jades and Light Greens

Jade × Jade ─────────────→ Olives and Jades

(Light Greens also should be produced in theory but the writer has not yet found this to be so in practice)

Olive × Jade ─────────────→ Olives and Jades

Olive × Olive ─────────────→ All Olives

The Dark factor makes it possible to produce Dark Pastel Blues (Single Dark factor Pastel Blues) and Slates (Double Dark factor Pastel Blues). The Dark Blues are the same to Pastel Blues as Jades are to Light Greens (Normals), and are darker in the same degree. Likewise the Slates are to Pastel Blues as Olives are to Light Greens; try to imagine a Pastel Blue darkened and with a grey cast, tinged slightly with sea-green; the face, forehead and throat are the same colour as in the Pastel Blue but the rump is slate grey with a slight mauve tinge. It is incorrect to refer to them as 'Cobalts' and 'Mauves' as they bear no resemblance to these colours in the Budgerigar.

To produce Dark Pastel Blues and Slates:

Pairing	Colour of Young
1 Olive × Pastel Blue ─────────→	**All Jades/Pastel Blue**
2 **Jade/Pastel Blue**	
× **Jade/Pastel Blue** ────────→	Light Greens (Normals), Light Greens/Pastel Blue, Pastel Blues, Jades, Jades/Pastel Blue, **Dark Pastel Blues (Single Dark factor Pastel Blues)**, Olives, Olives/Pastel Blue and Slates (**Double Dark factor Pastel Blues**)

The Pied Olive is quite attractive as the deep olive colour contrasts strongly with the yellow on wings and body, and the slate grey rump provides a strong contrast with the white flights. They are produced as follows:

Pairing	Colour of Young
1 Olive × Pied Light Green (Normal) →	Jades and **Pied Jades**
2 Olive × **Pied Jade** ────────→	Jades, Olives, Pied Jades and **Pied Olives**

Or

2 **Pied Jade** × **Pied Jade** ────────→	Jades, Olives, Pied Jades and **Pied Olives**

In producing Dark factor Dilutes, I have so far only completed the first cross which gives the necessary young to produce them next season; it can only be surmised what they will be like but it is hoped they will be something approaching a pale brown with a lime tinge.

To produce these the American Dilute must be used as the Japanese and Australian Dilutes will be too pale to show up the Dark factor in sufficient strength:

Pairing	Colour of Young
1 Olive × American Dilute ──────→	All Jades/American Dilute
2 **Jade/American Dilute**	
× **Jade/American Dilute** ──────→	Jades, Olives, Jades/American Dilute, Olives/American Dilute, **Single Dark factor American Dilutes** and **Double Dark factor American Dilutes**
Or	
2 **Jade/American Dilute**	
× American Dilute ──────→	Light Greens (Normals)/American Dilute, Jades/American Dilute American Dilutes and **Single Dark factor American Dilutes**
3 **Single Dark Factor American Dilute** × **Single Dark factor American Dilute** ──────→	Single Dark factor American Dilutes and **Double Dark factor American Dilutes**

Lutino

The Lutino mutation of the Peach-Faced originated in the aviaries of Mrs Mabel Schertzer of San Diego, California in 1970. This is the most strikingly beautiful of all lovebird mutations, being a rich golden yellow with red forehead, deep pink face and throat and white flights. The white rump is iridescent with blue lights, the tail is white and yellow and with carmine to dusky pink markings, the eyes are ruby red and the feet are pink.

The hatchlings are just like little red shrimps when they hatch; there is no mistaking them because, although of course their eyes are not open, there is no darkness beneath their lids and their eyes are pale flesh coloured. The primary down is sparser than that of non-Lutino Chicks.

Some hens will not accept them, ignoring their pleas for food, sometimes even mutilating them, all the time being model parents to the non-Lutinos in the nest. When these hens are found out it is wise to transfer the young Lutinos to nests where the mother has proven herself not to be belligerent towards red-eyed young.

78

The young have yellowish bills, the yellow areas of their plumage are slightly paler than they are in the adults and the pink areas much paler.

The mutation is sex-linked and works as follows:

Pairing	Colour of Young
Lutino cock × Normal hen ⟶	Normal cocks/Lutino and Lutino hens
Normal cock × Lutino hen ⟶	Normal cocks/Lutino and Normal hens
Normal cock/Lutino × Lutino hen ⟶	Lutino cocks, Lutino hens, Normal cocks/Lutino and Normal hens
Normal cock/Lutino × Normal hen ⟶	Lutino hens, Normal hens, Normal cocks/Lutino and Normal cocks
Lutino Cock × Lutino Hen ⟶	All Lutinos

N.B. A Normal hen *cannot* be split for a sex-linked colour.

Introduction of the Pied factor would have no visible effect on the Lutino, but a Pied Lutino (although the pied markings would be invisible) could result in a percentage of Pieds when paired with Normals, Pastel Blues and so on.

The introduction of the Dark, Cinnamon and Dilute factors would increase or lessen the depth of colour shown in the iridescent suffusion, particularly on the rump but this difference would only be evident to the practiced eye.

Cream Lutino

When the Pastel Blue factor is added to the Lutino a cream coloured bird with red eyes is produced. This Cream Lutino, (the term Cream Albino is incorrect), is reminiscent of the Yellow Faced Albino variety in Budgerigars.

It is buttermilk colour, yellowish on the wings, has a pale orange forehead, ivory blushed with pink throat, white flights, white tail with a trace of pink, iridescent white rump and, of course, ruby red eyes.

It can be produced thus:

Pairing	Colour of Young
ɪ Lutino cock × Pastel Blue hen ⟶	**Lutino hens/Pastel Blue and Cream Lutino**
	and
	Normal cocks/Pastel Blue, Lutino and Cream Lutino

79

**2 Normal cock/Pastel Blue,
Lutino and Cream
Lutino × Lutino hen/Pastel
Blue and Cream Lutino** ⟶ Lutino cocks, Lutino hens, Lutino
cocks/Pastel Blue and Cream Lutino,
Lutino hens/Pastel Blue and Cream
Lutino, Normal cocks/Pastel Blue,
Lutino and Cream Lutino, Normal
hens, Normal cocks/Lutino, Normal
hens/Pastel Blue, Pastel Blue cocks/
Cream Lutino, Pastel Blue hens,
Cream Lutino cocks and **Cream
Lutino hens**

Cinnamon

The Cinnamon Peach-Faced which originated in the USA is one of the newer mutations to become available. To the uninitiated they are not very striking and at first sight they could be mistaken for normal birds. A closer examination will show that they are quite attractive in a quiet, subtle way.

A Cinnamon Light (Normal) Green is a paler and softer shade of green with lighter blue rump; flights and tail markings are pale brown but the red and pink forehead, face and bib are the same as in the Normal Peach-Faced. Their feet and nails are paler coloured than those of Normals.

Cinnamon characteristics are sex-linked and the factor can be combined with Pastel Blue, the Dark factor, the Dilute factors and their combinations which it will serve to lighten and soften. When combined with the Pied factor it will only lighten those areas of the birds' plumage which are unaffected by the Pied factor, while those areas which are variegated will remain the same as they would be if the bird did not possess the Cinnamon factor.

There would be no real advantage in combining Cinnamon with Lutino as the only difference to be seen would be in the iridescent suffusion.

Cinnamon Pastel Blues can be produced as follows:

Pairing	Colour of Young
1 Cinnamon Normal cock × Pastel Blue hen ⟶	**Normal cocks/Cinnamon and Pastel Blue** and **Cinnamon Normal hens/Pastel Blue**

80

2 **Normal cock/Cinnamon and**
   Pastel Blue × Cinnamon
   Normal hen/Pastel Blue ———→ Normal hens, Normal
   cocks/Cinnamon, Cinnamon hens,
   Cinnamon cocks, Normal hens/Pastel
   Blue, Normal cocks/Cinnamon and
   Pastel Blue, Cinnamon hens/Pastel
   Blue, Pastel Blue hens, Pastel Blue
   cocks/Cinnamon, **Cinnamon Pastel**
   Blue hens and **Cinnamon Pastel**
   Blue cocks

Or

2 **Normal cock/Cinnamon and**
   Pastel Blue × Pastel Blue hen ———→ Normal hens/Pastel Blue, Normal
   cocks/Pastel Blue, Cinnamon
   hens/Pastel Blue, Normal
   cocks/Cinnamon and Pastel Blue,
   Pastel Blue hens, Pastel Blue cocks,
   Cinnamon Pastel Blue hens and
   Pastel Blue cocks/Cinnamon

To provide a formula to produce Cinnamon Dilutes simply replace
'Pastel Blue' with 'Dilute' in the above.
To produce Cinnamon Olives:

Pairing	**Colour of Young**
1 Cinnamon Normal cock	
× Olive hen ——————————→	**Cinnamon Jade hens** and **Jade** **cocks/Cinnamon**
2 **Jade cock/Cinnamon**	
× **Cinnamon Jade hen** ———→	Jade hens, Jade cocks/Cinnamon, Cinnamon Jade hens, Cinnamon Jade cocks, Olive hens, Olive cocks/Cinnamon, **Cinnamon Olive** **hens** and **Cinnamon Olive cocks**

To produce Cinnamon Pieds:

Pairing	**Colour of Young**
Cinnamon Normal cock × Single Pied Hen ——————————→	Cinnamon Normal hens, Normal cocks/Cinnamon, **Single Pied** **Cinnamon hens** and Single Pied cocks/Cinnamon

Red Suffusion

From time to time a bird appears with a red suffusion over part of
or over its entire body excepting the rump.
   In a Normal Peach-Faced this red overlay gives the bird a muddy

red appearance but when this condition occurs with a Pied of high yellow variegation or a Dilute, then a very pleasing dusky pink effect is obtained.

So far no true breeding strains have been established.

It has been said that this mutant can be caused by a lack of some element in its diet which may be so with some specimens. However, this colour has been produced in birds of the second generation in my aviaries which must prove that it is worthwhile to persevere.

Other Mutant Peach-Faced

The only other mutant factor to be reported on to date is a White Faced Blue. If this is correct and this new mutant is a true blue mutation showing no trace of green or pink, as the Pastel Blue does, then by combining with the other factors many new colours can be produced. For example, Pure White Albinos, Pied Blues (with pure white and blue contrasts), Pale Silvers (Dilute White Faced Blues), Cinnamon White Faced Blues, and Dark Greys (Double Dark factor White Faced Blues) which would be grey with a white face, dark grey rump and almost black flights and tail. It can easily be imagined what other beautiful and unusual colours and varieties could be produced by combining these factors still further. If, as is hoped, the White Faced Blue does already exist, in all probability it will be a straight forward recessive.

So we can now produce colours which combine the Double Dark, Dilute, Cinnamon, Pied, Pastel Blue and Lutino factors in various permutations. Of course, the appearance of these combinations may not even merit the trouble of producing them but, by experimenting, something worthwhile may result or at least our suppositions will be proved correct. Even if some of these combination colours do not have an attractive appearance they still have a use. When paired to the correct mate they could be used to produce nests of young of various colours, the combination colours being split into the primary factors, or alternative combinations of colours, much as a glass prism breaks up sunlight into the colours of the rainbow.

As an example of combining mutations, think of the beautiful and scintillating colours of the Rainbow Budgerigar which combines the Yellow Faced, Opaline, Whitewing, Single Dark and Blue factors with the Violet factor as an added option. Attention to feather quality is required to give this variety added brilliance and sparkle from light refraction. In Australia further development is being carried out on dilutes where Yellow Rumped and White Rumped Australian Dilutes are being bred.

5   Breeding Problems

The first problem to be met with is that of *selecting a true pair*. This does not of course apply to those species showing sexual dimorphism but it is, unfortunately, another matter with the rest of the genus and boils down to a matter of intelligent guesswork, trial and error, and good luck! The only proof of a true pair is fertile eggs. Birds can be tried together in pairs or, as long as they are watched, in small groups of four to six and, as they form attachments, transferred to small breeding pens.

Incompatibility can occur with fully adult true pairs in which case the quarrelling birds should be split up and reintroduced in a few days time when they may be in a more receptive mood, their disposition completely changed.

Infertility sometimes occurs but seldom lasts for more than one round of eggs and just shows that one of the partners is off condition

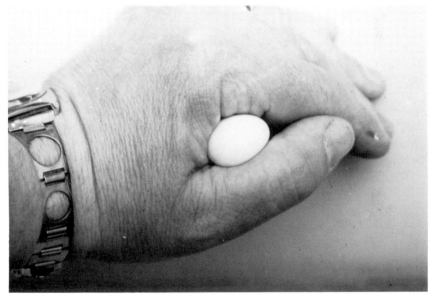

Holding eggs up to a strong source of light will allow you to see if the embryo is developing.

temporarily. Eggs can be tested for fertility by holding them up to the light against the eye; usually by the time the fourth egg is laid the first one will be already darkening very slightly.

Eggbinding is caused by a sudden cold spell giving the hen cramp, by an ill-formed or rough egg and sometimes, very rarely, by an

83

extremely large egg. The affected hen is found in a collapsed state, breathing rapidly and in obvious discomfort. In order to save the bird no time must be lost in placing her in a hospital cage or something similar, providing comforting warmth of 80°–90°F. A little warm olive oil should be run down inside the vent. Hens which are not quite mature are prone to eggbinding if encouraged to nest too quickly.

Soft shelled eggs can be the result of breeding with immature hens and also indicate a lack of sufficient intake of calcium. If an egg breaks inside a hen death is usually very rapid. However, if the birds have a continuous supply of cuttlefish bone and immature birds are not rushed into breeding, problems with the making and laying of eggs are unlikely to occur.

Cracked or chipped eggs provided they are only slighlty damaged can be repaired with a coat or two of nail varnish; this is very often successful and the egg will develop and hatch normally so long as no microbes have already entered the interior.

Chicks clearing the eggshells. If young are having difficulty then some careful help can be given, but it is best to leave eggs which are just 'pipping' to hatch by themselves; frequently a chick will take two days from first chipping the egg shell to emerging and if you pull out the chick too soon it will not have absorbed all the yolk and will die. If egg shells are left in the nest these can sometimes cover and stick to unhatched eggs and prevent the young from emerging.

Parents leaving the nest at night. A nesting pair may sometimes be drawn off the nest at night for a variety of reasons, such as extra bright moonlight, gales, cats, and so on. If this happens try to coax them back into the nest by shining a torch onto the nesthole and with a little patience a steady pair will go back.

Should it be impossible to persuade them, never catch them and force them into the box, they will only panic and shoot out again. Never, ever put them in and block the hole or eggs and young will be trampled and only one of the parent birds will be found alive at daybreak.

If they refuse, or at least the hen refuses to return to the nest, the eggs may not be spoiled if the night is mild; in the case of youngsters well below fledging age, it is best to remove them to a warm place, handfeeding them through the night if necessary, and replacing them in their nest at daybreak.

All species will not take this interference, but if the night is particularly cold it is worth the chance. The Peach-Faced are most tolerant and will generally carry on caring for their young in spite of interference and nest inspections.

Handfeeding. In the case of nests being deserted it is possible to foster out the eggs or young to other pairs. The Peach-Faced are the most tolerant of this practice.

If all else fails it may be necessary to handfeed the young until foster parents can be persuaded to take to them. Lovebird chicks of only a few hours old can be persuaded to suck warm food from a small teaspoon. If preferred, and the young are old enough to take it, food can be injected into the crop via a hypodermic syringe with tube attached. The tube must be inserted down the throat and right into the crop before the food is ejected. Care must be taken not to bruise the tender young membranes of the throat and crop.

Lovebird chicks will suck warm food from a spoon. (Children enjoy seeing baby lovebirds grow and the Peach-Faced are an ideal species with which to initiate them into the hobby of bird breeding.)

If the chicks are to be taken away from their parents and will be receiving their entire nourishment by handfeeding, then finely chopped sunflower seed with a little brown bread, milk and added vitamins should be used. This should be mixed to a porridgy consistency with water and given very warm. Young birds will not take cold food but will eagerly suck warm food from a teaspoon. They must be fed enough times to keep their crops from being completely empty at any time but not over bloated and tightly distended. With

85

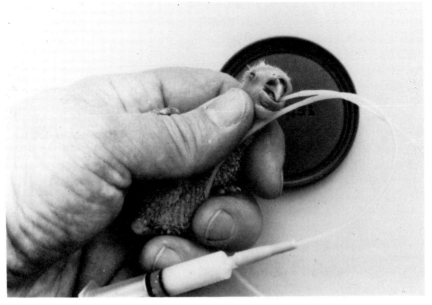
Lovebird chicks can be fed by means of a tube and syringe.

very young birds it is necessary to feed them several times through the night. Older birds can be fed at about 12 p.m. and then left until 6 a.m. for the first feed of the day. They should be fed a further four to five times throughout the day.

If the handfeeding is to be merely supplementary, perhaps two or three times a day to a chick which is much smaller than its nestmates and is not getting its fair share, then the food to use is 'Farex' baby cereal. Mix the 'Farex' cereal with warm water to a thin enough consistency to be sucked up into a syringe. A pinch of vitamin/mineral powder can be added as the young progress.

The chicks must be kept warm and dry. Hatchlings need to be kept at 29°–32°C (85°–90°F) so a small incubator or a thermostatically controlled hospital cage is required until they are sufficiently developed to be kept at room temperature. The heat is required to promote the correct rate of growth and digestion. (Their droppings are much more watery when being handfed.) The older the chicks are at the time handfeeding begins the more likely they are to be successfully reared.

It is not recommended that breeding operations of all the species of lovebirds be disrupted but with the Peach-Faced it is possible to examine the nest daily and to examine the young to make sure they

86

are being fed sufficiently. With large nests of Peach-Faced, the smallest and weakest are very often fed barely enough to keep them alive; they should be handfed two or three times daily to supplement the little food they get from their parents until they are strong enough to demand their due.

When the young are large, supplementary handfeeding with 'Farex' directly causes the nests to become very wet and unpleasant which will attract fodder mite; to prevent this the nest must be cleaned out as often as necessary and refurbished with a dry bed of used millet sprays or similar. Never use fine hay, this could contain cultures of harmful moulds which will flourish in the warm, damp conditions of the nestbox.

Plucked young are often the direct result of the irritation of *fodder mite* caused to parents and babies while in the nest. Fodder mite need moisture to survive so any damp patch of spilled food will nourish them and encourage them to thrive. They can be seen as fawnish grey clusters which, if left, will soon increase in size to a whole shovel full. From here, individuals will move up the woodwork of the flight and into the nests.

The mite should be removed and burned, the floor where they were should be sprinkled with paraffin and the woodwork painted over

Young which have been plucked on the back soon re-grow their feathers on fledging.

Fodder mite.

with it. If possible, the nestboxes should be gone over with a blowlamp.

Alugan (Hoechst (UK) Ltd) is an insecticide and an acaricide (effective against mites). A solution of this is used to paint the woodwork of the flights and is said to eradicate the mite after several applications spaced a few weeks apart. Consult your vet regarding the correct strength to use and the risk of any toxic effect Alugan might have on your birds.

If adults persist in plucking their young they should be fostered out before serious damage is done to the flesh of their wings, backs and heads. Continual supply of twigs and branches will often draw the unwelcome attention of the parents away from the young which may be plucked for nesting material.

6   Health Problems

If your lovebirds are kept under the conditions required by each species health problems will be few. The most susceptible are, of course, the smaller, weaker species which are more prone to chills and pneumonia being less resistant to cold and damp foggy weather.

It is impossible to list and deal with all possible eventualities that could arise and in any case there are excellent text books dealing solely with the diseases of cage and aviary birds, so only the few most commonly arising complaints will be covered.

Warmth is required to assist the recovery of sick birds from most ailments so it is necessary to own a hospital cage in which the heat can be thermostatically controlled. Better than a hospital cage is a small room with a thermostat and heater installed where sick birds can convalesce in roomy flight cages. The heat should be adjusted to a temperature at which the bird looks comfortable; for a very sick bird the thermostat should be set at 27°–32°C (80°–90° F). In a room the sickest birds should be placed at a high point where they will benefit from the extra warmth while those improving can be placed progressively lower.

As the bird recovers the heat can be reduced a few degrees each day until the temperature is down to the range that the bird is used to in its usual environment in the aviary or bird room.

With most illnesses it is essential to provide light through the evening as well as the day to encourage the sick bird to drink and eat frequently throughout the night so replacing its energy and body fluids previously lost and giving it the necessary strength to fight off its debility.

Chills and enteritis are the most common ailments. It would be difficult to distinguish between the two. In both cases the bird is found in a distressed condition with feathers fluffed out, droppings are watery and the crop is generally empty of food. If left the bird will deteriorate and die in a short time. The sick bird may be found in a collapsed state, barely alive, in which case immediate exposure to warmth may still bring the bird around.

With experience it is possible to pick out birds that are becoming ill by their lethargic appearance when they are unaware of being watched, closing of eyes, uninterest in the seed dish at feeding time and failing to go to roost in their usual place.

Infectious Enteritis. Warmth is generally all that is needed to cure the above conditions but in case of an infectious enteritis it is wise to put the bird on an antibiotic for five days. Aureomycin (chlortetracycline hydrochloride) can be given in their drinking water, just enough of the powder to turn it a little green. (If you are unsure it is wise to ask the vet what amount he would recommend you should use.) It is unwise to give the affected bird any green food as this will increase the scouring.

If the bird is reluctant to eat it may be necessary to handfeed it by use of a hypodermic syringe with tube attached so injecting the food straight into the crop in the same manner as will be described for de-worming. 'Farex' with a little vitamin and mineral powder and a little antibiotic mixed with warm water to a consistency which can be drawn up into the syringe is the food which should be given. One or two millilitres should be given at each feed (about three hours apart) until the bird is able to feed itself.

Pneumonia. Should a chill turn to pneumonia and the bird commence to gasp, very little can be done to save it though we have had success on occasion by administering 'Penbritin' (ampicillin), Beecham Animal Health, and of course keeping the bird in heat.

'Penbritin' can be obtained in a paste form supplied in ready to use oral dosers with long thin nozzles which can be inserted between the bird's mandibles and a little of the substance ejected into the bird's mouth, most of this will be swallowed by the patient.

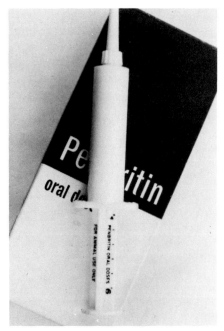

Penbritin is available in handy applicator.

90

Paralysis is, initially, the symptom of an illness or deficiency of some particular vitamins and/or minerals. If the problem causing the paralysis can be discovered and put to rights the paralysis will frequently disappear but if it persists it is possible to get rid of it, to some extent at least.

The bird is found lying on the floor or gripping onto the wire with its bill, with toes, feet, legs and sometimes wings in a rigid state. Sometimes only one leg or a couple of toes are affected. If the toe nails are examined, small red blotches will be seen in the vein as if blood vessels have burst or a clotting of the blood has blocked the vein. These blotches later turn blackish.

Warmth, antibiotic, vitamin and mineral treatments are required. All food should be placed in shallow dishes on the floor of the cage so as the crippled bird can reach it.

Regular and frequent massage and manipulation of legs and toes will in nine cases out of ten effect at least a partial recovery. Spirits of iodine or even methylated spirits should be used as a rub to help stimulate the nerves in the deadened limbs. The use will come back into the wings shortly after the fit preceeding the paralysis.

Sour crop is prevalent in sultry weather and to help prevent it, water receptacles should be cleaned and replenished daily. Two teaspoons of bicarbonate of soda to a pint of water given to drink once a week in hot weather also helps prevent the condition. It is unlikely that this treated water would be harmful to freshly hatched young, but as a precaution, I have withheld it from those pairs with young of two or three days old.

A bird affected with sour crop will be seen to be in obvious distress, its crop blown up with a smelly, stagnant, watery content. At the slightest pressure on the crop the contents will trickle from the bird's mouth as a frothy liquid.

Most birds can be cured of this condition by using the following method. (Sometimes, they may die while this treatment is being carried out but they will most definitely die if nothing is done to alleviate their distress.) The crop must be stripped of its putrid content by gently manipulating it with thumb and forefinger and ejecting it from the bird's mouth. It will also run from the bird's nostrils. It is imperative to hold the bird head down during the entire operation of stripping and cleansing the crop, otherwise the liquid will get into its lungs and drown it.

The crop should be cleansed by flushing out with a solution of one teaspoon of bicarbonate of soda to a quarter of a cup of warm water by using a syringe with tube fitted (as previously described). The tube must be gently worked down the bird's throat and into its crop, the solution ejected into the crop and, (all the while holding the bird head down), gently squeeze out the cleansing solution till it pours back out of the bird's mouth. This must be done three or four times to make sure the crop is well flushed out. Wipe the bird's face, and with a clean tube and syringe, feed it with a mixture of Farex (Farley Health Laboratories), water, a little vitamin powder and a little antibiotic as previously described. This treatment may need to be carried out two or three times a day before the sourness of the crop ceases to return, and perhaps over a period of two or three days.

Eye infections are not very common with lovebirds, but, in the case of such an occurrence, obtain a suitable antibiotic eye ointment from your vet and apply it to the eye once or twice a day for the recommended number of days, not just until the soreness has disappeared. Pull down the bird's eyelid, squeeze some of the ointment into it allowing it to melt and run around the eye and lid.

Aureomycin eye ointment (Cyanamid) is generally prescribed and usually proves effective. In the case of particularly stubborn infections, neomycin sulphate, Neobiotic eye ointment (Upjohn Ltd), has cleared them. Your vet may suggest that the birds are treated orally with the same antibiotic as is in the eye ointment. They should also be given a vitamin and mineral supplement.

Keep any affected birds in isolation for a time in case of a contagious disease which could be transmitted to the rest of your stock.

Small wounds on feet, legs, bills, and so on are quite common and, though they usually heal quite rapidly on their own, can be dusted over with an antibiotic powder. The loss of a nail or even the tip of a toe is generally taken in the bird's stride and discomfort is shown by the bird for only an hour or so. In extreme cold weather wounded (or frostbitten) birds should be taken into the warm or the wound will not stop bleeding. If left outside the bird will continue to bite the wound as the cold has numbed all feeling.

Bills and nails which have become overgrown or deformed can be clipped back into shape with nail clippers; just be careful not to cut too high, into a vein.

Wryneck or vertigo is a condition generally preceded by a fit. The bird is found twisting its head right round and is unable to hold it normally. It cannot maintain its balance nor control the direction of its flight. This condition may be caused by an infection, damage to the nervous system or maybe simply by mites having crawled inside the birds ear.

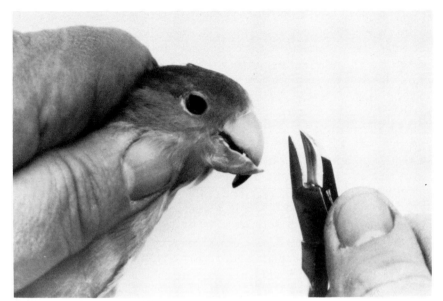
Cutting a severly overgrown bill.

To cover all eventualities the bird should be dusted over with an anti-mite powder, be put in a warm, quiet place with subdued lighting; treated with an antibiotic in the drinking water and given vitamins and minerals. A tiny amount of Earex (as used for earache in humans) should be dropped into each ear hole everyday until the problem subsides which it generally does in a matter of a few weeks. Usually the bird is left with a slight imbalance, a tendency to pull to one side with its head and in its flight.

Pasteurella or Pseudotuberculosis is an insidious disease spread by rodents and wild birds, in particular Greenfinches and Sparrows. It is prevalent in cold and damp weather, and can only be diagnosed after a post mortem examination and bacterial tests. Of the various symptoms indicative of the disease the most common is the discolouration (pallid) of the liver, spleen and other internal organs and presence of lesions and yellowish white spots and abcesses in these organs. The gut is often full of undigested blood.

The victim dies very quickly with very few external symptoms, the droppings are normal, the bird shows a slight malaise, glazing of the eyes and lack of appetite. The bird dies in a fit as the toxic agents released by the disease quickly poison it.

If the disease is suspected, veterinary advice should be sought immediately as it may be possible to prevent the disease spreading to other stock or to save other birds incubating the disease by treatment with a specific antibiotic.

Feather plucking is common enough with larger parrots, though not so frequent among adult lovebirds. Sometimes if they are so inclined treatment with the anti-peck aerosol sprays, together with provision of extra branches and twigs to keep their bills occupied helps to check the habit.

Mite of various species are a pest but can be easily kept down by using the various anti-mite sprays, painting the woodwork with paraffin and burning out nestboxes with a blowlamp.

Moulds are a definite health hazard, they thrive on damp concrete and in stale food, and are responsible for lung disorders such as aspergillosis.

Rats are a problem that is easily solved. They can be kept out of the flights by the method already described under 'Suitable Housing' in the first chapter.

Mice are a different matter. They can pass through the smallest gap and will quickly colonise your aviaries and spread disease.

Warfarin (Boots Chemicals) is not now a dependable rodenticide as rats and mice quickly become immune to it. We have found that 'Ratak' (ICI), with active constituent ifenacoum, is most suitable as long as it is used in accordance with the instructions and will wipe out firmly established colonies of rodents. Evidence that the vermin are taking the bait is shown in their droppings which are dyed a vivid green from the ingestion of the green 'Ratak' pellets. Care must be taken that the 'Ratak' pellets cannot be carried into aviaries where birds can pick them up.

Roundworms are the cause of death of many parrot-like birds and lovebirds are not immune to their invasion. The worms debilitate their victims by living off the food passing through their intestines, causing irritation and inflamation, and finally killing them by causing a blockage in and rupturing the gut. It is, however, a simple job for the person who is confident in handling his birds, to dose them with a reliable de-worming agent straight into their crops by using the method described on page 96. It is possible, but not preferable, to dose them by adding the chemical to their drinking water; this is not a sure way as the birds may not drink enough, if any, of the treated water once tasted.

Roundworms which have been passed after deworming.

Roundworms hatch out in the bird's gut from eggs which are picked up as it feeds; they are like earthworms in appearance but much thinner and can grow in the bird's intestines to a length exceeding two inches. The parasite lays its eggs while in its host, these are passed out in the bird's excrement and so the cycle continues.

The eggs, which are only visible through a microscope, are very tough and can only be destroyed by going over the entire flight with a flame gun or blow lamp. Those that are exposed to long periods of direct sunlight will be destroyed but those protected in shady, damp positions can survive to perpetuate the adult parasite. Many wild British birds suffer from worms, so this is another source of worm eggs which can be transferred to your stock as wild birds hop around on the roof of your aviary.

95

Unnecessary mortality can be avoided by de-worming the stock at fairly regular intervals, say, in the autumn, mid-winter, spring and summer. Young birds should be de-wormed at weaning age.

If worms are found in the droppings the bird so affected should be dosed again three weeks later. The de-worming programme is carried out each year regardless of evidence or non-evidence of infestation as a preventative measure.

'Nilverm' (ICI) is a very efficient de-worming agent which we have been using for many years and have found to have no detrimental effect on the health and fertility of our stock. Made specifically for use on farmstock, Nilverm can be obtained in a solution, and can be purchased from your local vet. It is generally only available in quite a large pack which, as such a small amount is required to do the job, will last the average breeder for several years during which time Nilverm will not deteriorate nor lose its potency, provided it is kept tightly sealed, away from heat and out of light. Nilverm should be diluted, one part Nilverm to four parts water. Half a millilitre of this solution is a suitable dosage for a lovebird. This solution can be given orally by using a hypodermic syringe and small size (2 mm wide) dog catheter tube. Disposable syringes and catheter tubes can be obtained from your vet. At the end of the catheter tube, on each side, there are two

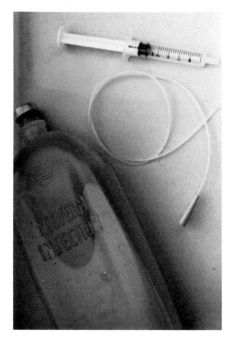

Catheter tube, syringe and Nilverm – all
that is required to keep losses through
roundworms to a minimum.

holes. Cut off the end of the tube just above the highest hole, smooth off the end of the cut tube by holding briefly in a naked flame.

It is best to de-worm the birds early so that the day's activity will help move the worms through the intestines; if it is left until evening when the birds would soon be going to roost a heavy accumulation of worms during the night could cause a blockage of the gut.

The following information on holding the bird and manipulating the tube down the bird's throat is applicable for the other occasions mentioned in this book when a syringe and tube are recommended to be used, in handfeeding, and administering medicine.

The bird to be de-wormed should be caught with the minimum, of fuss and, when caught, care should be taken not to constrict the abdomen so as to prevent breathing. Hold the bird so that it cannot peck you or you may damage it by a reflex action! Hold it with its back in the palm of your hand and firmly, without squeezing, hold its head still by placing the index finger on top of its head, thumb and second finger each side of its head below the eyes.

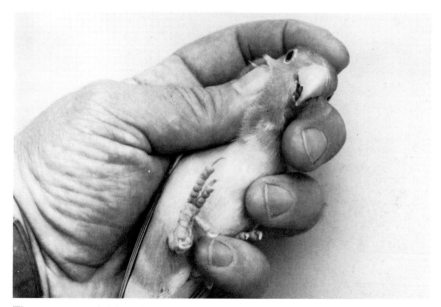

The correct way to hold an adult bird.

Now, with the bird held safely in the left hand, the right hand is free to manipulate the tube into the corner of the bird's mouth, over the tongue and down the throat. If it does not slip straight down into the crop do not force it but gently work it back and forth until you can

97

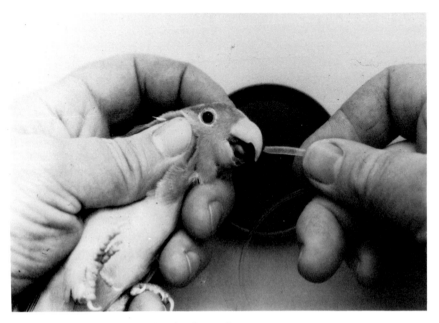

Insert the tube into the corner of the bird's mouth.

Manipulate the tube down the throat into the crop.

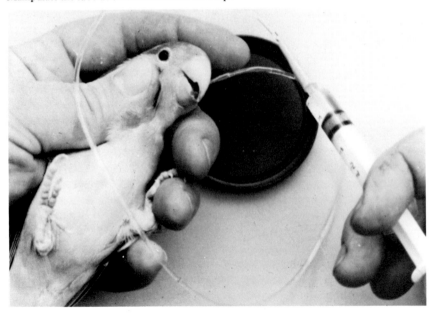

feel no obstruction. (It is imperative the tube goes right into the crop and not just into the throat.) Even greater care must be taken with young birds as the skin inside the mouth, throat and crop is tender and any rough handling can cause bleeding. If this does happen release the bird and try again another day.

Once the tube is well into the crop, eject the Nilvern slowly from the syringe and not with a sharp spurt. If any choking occurs or liquid bubbles from the nostrils, release the bird immediately so it is able to cough up the liquid which has obviously gone down the wrong way; try again later. Be warned that it is *possible* to mistakenly introduce the tube down into the birds windpipe so that the ejected liquid floods the lungs and the bird drowns. To guard against this happening make sure that you can feel the end of the inserted tube inside the bird's crop before emptying the contents of the syringe.

After the chemical has been administered correctly, the bird can be shut in a shelter or a cage with newspaper under the perches, so that evidence of the destruction of the pests can be clearly seen and disposed of. Worms are usually passed four to five hours after dosing, but sometimes not until the next day. For further reference, do not forget to make note of the date when each individual specimen was treated.

The syringe and tube can be sterilized by boiling after dosing each pair or group of birds; failing this, the tube can be cleansed with a cloth impregnated with a mild antiseptic solution to help stop transmitting any undetected bacterial infections through the entire stock.

When purchasing new stock always find out if they have been de-wormed recently and if worms were present. If they have not been treated, let them settle in for a day or so before dosing them.

How to Identify Causes of Death

If, as sometimes happens, a bird is found dead then a number of facts can be discovered by a quick examination of the body. These facts may point to a simple reason for the bird's death.

Some things to look for:

1 Feel the crop to see if it is empty (perhaps it has been kept from food by its mate), has food in it, or is full of liquid (sourcrop?).

2 Feel the flesh on each side of the breast bone to see if the bird is plump or if it is thin and 'gone light' which indicates disease.

3 Feel the neck for any breaks, indicating an accident.

4 Examine the vent. Is it wet and dirty, is there a trace of blood which could indicate enteritis, haemorrhage or rupture of the gut due to worms?

5   Examine the body for any large yellowish lumps which may be growths.

6   Examine the head, feet and abdomen for any marks which may have been caused by fighting.

7   Examine the eyes, bill and, particularly, the nostrils for any discharge which may indicate bacterial or viral infection of the respiratory or digestive tracts.

8   Pluck away the feathers from the neck and examine the windpipe (indicated by its rings of cartilage) for a blockage of mucus, traces of mite, etc.

9   Pluck off the feathers from the scalp and examine the skull for damage such as blood clots or haemorrhage, indicating an accident or fit.

Skull of lovebird shows no damage or haemorrhage.

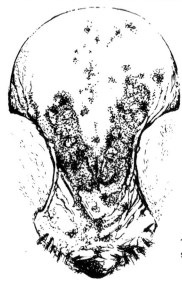

Top of skull of Grass Parrakeet; dark areas show massive haemorrhage.

After noting the above and if no simple explanation for the death emerges you may wish to take the body to a vet for a post mortem or you may be curious to examine the bird internally yourself.

Remember that once the bird has been opened up it will probably not be possible for you to pass it on to a vet for clinical tests; there is also a risk, however miniscule, of contracting one of those diseases which are communicable from birds to man.

To be able to discern between healthy and diseased organs it is necessary to be familiar with the usual healthy appearance of the bird's vital organs by opening up those birds that have died due to fighting and accident.

This is a suitable way of opening up the bird followed by some points to look for:

a)   Lay the bird on a sheet of newspaper, pluck off all the feathers from the abdomen (noting if there are any external parasites) and put them into a paper bag to prevent them being blown around.

b)   With a sharp craft knife or scalpel cut through the tissue just beneath the keel bone and through the lower ribs, pull up the breast bone leaving the internal organs laid out for easy viewing.

c)   Note if the body cavities are full of blood and liquid which may

Post Mortem – Pluck off feathers.   Cut, and lift up keel bone.

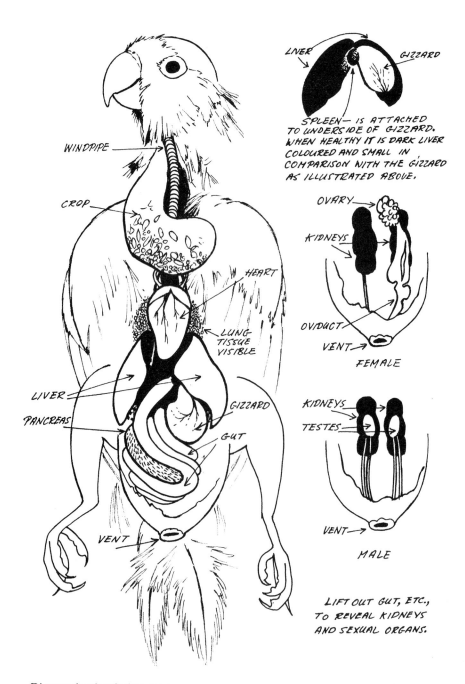

WINDPIPE

CROP

LIVER

PANCREAS

VENT

HEART

LUNG TISSUE VISIBLE

GIZZARD

GUT

LIVER

GIZZARD

SPLEEN— IS ATTACHED TO UNDERSIDE OF GIZZARD. WHEN HEALTHY IT IS DARK LIVER COLOURED AND SMALL IN COMPARISON WITH THE GIZZARD AS ILLUSTRATED ABOVE.

OVARY

KIDNEYS

OVIDUCT

VENT

FEMALE

KIDNEYS

TESTES

VENT

MALE

LIFT OUT GUT, ETC., TO REVEAL KIDNEYS AND SEXUAL ORGANS.

Diagram showing the internal organs.

indicate a haemorrhage, or rupture of the gut due to worms.

d) Examine the liver and spleen for abnormal size and discolouration (pallid, yellowish, pinkish) also for spots, nodules (of a white or yellow colour) and lesions which indicates disease or a disorder. (e.g. pseudotuberculosis, hepatitis).

e) Examine the heart for deposits of blood which may indicate a burst artery due to shock and stress.

f) Examine gut for undigested blood content indicating various diseases, the commonest being enteritis of an infectious nature.

g) Examine the gut for evidence of rupture and for parasitical worms.

h) Examine the lower gut near the vent for hard, solid deposits of excreta indicating severe constipation.

i) Examine (in case of breeding hens) for trace of ruptured egg sack, malformed egg and so on.

j) Examine lungs for abcesses, lesions, and mucus.

h) Examine the gizzard (the round, solid, muscular organ in the digestive tract) for bloating. Sometimes it will become distended and blocked. Cut it in half to see if there is contained sufficient grit or too much grit and what the other contents are.

When you are satisfied with your findings, dispose of the remains by burning, wash and disinfect your hands and the blade. If you have found something you are worried by then consult your vet.

Addenda

Abyssinian Lovebirds

As mutant Abyssinian lovebirds are rare, and to complete the information on mutations known to me, I feel it is worth recording that I once owned a Cinnamon Abyssinian cock. This bird apparently originated from a consignment of birds caught wild in Ethiopia and was obtained from Mr John Wood's establishment near Cheltenham. This bird had pale lime plumage, brown flights, paler bill but, unusually, retained the black underwing coverts. Mr George Smith of Peterborough bred some cocks from this bird but no headway was made in founding a strain and it is supposed that the line has now disappeared.

Masked Lovebirds

The following colour expectations in the combination of Blue and Yellow factors are supplementary to those listed on pages 59 and 60:

Cross		Expectation
Normal/Blue, Yellow and White × Blue/White	⟶	Normals/Blue, Normals/White, Blues, Blues/White, Yellows/White and Whites
Normal/Blue, Yellow and White × Yellow/White	⟶	Normals/Yellow, Normals/White, Blues/White, Yellows, Yellows/White and Whites
Blue/White × Yellow	⟶	Normals/White and Yellows/White
Blue/White × Yellow/White	⟶	Normals/White, Yellow/White, Blues/White and Whites
Blue/White × Blue/White	⟶	Blues, Blues/White and Whites
Blue/White × Blue	⟶	Blues and Blues/White
Yellow/White × Yellow/White	⟶	Yellows, Yellows/White and Whites
Yellow/White × Yellow	⟶	Yellows and Yellows/White
Yellow/White × Blue	⟶	Normals/White and Blues/White

N.B. In the right hand column Normal/White is an abbreviation for Normal/Blue, Yellow and White. (A Normal/White carries the blue and yellow factors.)

Acknowledgements

I should like to thank the following friends for allowing me to photograph their birds for some of the plates in this book: Mrs June Smith of Swindon (Madagascar, Yellow Fischer's, Yellow Masked and White Masked lovebirds); Mr B. W. Tanner of Kencot (Normal Masked, Normal Fischer's, and Abyssinian lovebirds) and Mr Fred Garfield of Broad Hembury (Red-faced lovebirds).

Many thanks are due to Mr Fred Garfield for information on breeding Red-Faced lovebirds; also to Mr J. J. Postema of the Netherlands for information on his Lutino and Albino Masked lovebirds.

Index

Figures in **bold** type are plate numbers in the colour section.